THE
ONLY CHILD

Center Point
Large Print

Also by Andrew Pyper and available from Center Point Large Print:

The Damned

This Large Print Book carries the Seal of Approval of N.A.V.H.

THE
ONLY
CHILD

ANDREW
PYPER

CENTER POINT LARGE PRINT
THORNDIKE, MAINE

This Center Point Large Print edition
is published in the year 2017 by arrangement with
Simon & Schuster, Inc.

The text of this Large Print edition is unabridged.
In other aspects, this book may vary
from the original edition.
Printed in the United States of America
on permanent paper.
Set in 16-point Times New Roman type.

ISBN: 978-1-68324-473-8

Library of Congress Cataloging-in-Publication Data

Names: Pyper, Andrew, author.
Title: The only child / Andrew Pyper.
Description: Center Point Large Print edition. | Thorndike, Maine :
    Center Point Large Print, 2017.
Identifiers: LCCN 2017021929 | ISBN 9781683244738
    (hardcover : alk. paper)
Subjects: LCSH: Forensic psychiatrists—Fiction. | Large type books. |
GSAFD: Suspense fiction.
Classification: LCC PR9199.3.P96 O55 2017 | DDC 813/.54—dc23
LC record available at https://lccn.loc.gov/2017021929

To Heidi, Maude, and Ford

Do you not think that there are things which you cannot understand, and yet which are; that some people see things that others cannot? . . . Ah, it is the fault of our science that it wants to explain all; and if it explain not, then it says there is nothing to explain.

—Bram Stoker, *Dracula*

PART 1

The New World

1

She was awakened by the monster knocking at the door.

Lily knows better than most how unlikely it is that this is real. Through her years of training and now her days in the courtroom providing expert testimony on psychological states of mind, she has learned how shaky the recollections of children can be. And she was only six when it happened. The age when certain things get stuck in the net of real memory, and other things you try to sell yourself on having happened but are in fact made up, turned into convincing bits of dream.

What is verifiably known is that Lily was small for her age, green-eyed, her straight black hair snarled into a nest. The sole survivor. And there was the body, of course. Her mother's.

She rereads the documents the authorities submitted the same way others return to old love letters or family photo albums, tracing the outlines of faces. It's an act of remembrance, but something more too. She's looking for the missing link. Because though the coroner and police reports seem decisive enough, plausible enough, she can see all the ways the facts were stretched to connect to other facts with long strings of theory in between. It was a story assembled to close a file. A terrible, but not unprecedented, northern tale of an animal attack: a creature of considerable size—a bear, almost certainly, drawn by scents of cooked meat and human sweat—had forced its way into their cabin a couple hundred miles short of the Arctic Circle in Alaska and torn her mother apart, leaving Lily undiscovered in her bedroom, where she'd hidden from the screams.

Acceptable on the face of it, as such stories are designed to be. Yet there was so much that wasn't known it made for a narrative that collapsed upon itself at the merest prodding. Why, for instance, had the bear not eaten her mother? Where could it have gone that the hunters who went after it only a day later failed to find its tracks?

The most puzzling part was how she made it out of the woods.

Three miles to the only road that led, after a two-hour drive, to Fairbanks. The trail to the cabin a set of muddy ruts in summer, but in the subzero depths of February impossible to reach except by snowmobile, and her mother's Kawasaki remained untouched at the site. When and why did she eventually leave the cabin? How did she get through the woods all on her own?

The year she turned thirty Lily spent her summer vacation conducting an investigation of her own. She traveled north to see the cabin for herself and walked from the site through an aspen forest to the rusting trailer her mother had called their "secret place." She spoke with all the people she could find who were mentioned in the reports.

That was how she came to meet one of the hunters who'd assisted on the case. An old man by the time she took a seat next to the bed where he lay in an old-age home for Native Americans in Anchorage. A man old enough to have nothing to lose and grateful for the visit of a young woman.

"My name is Lily," she told him. "Lily Dominick? When I was a girl—"

"I remember you."

"You do?"

"The one the bear didn't touch." He shook his head with a kind of sad amusement, as if at the recollection of a practical joke gone wrong. "Except it wasn't a bear."

"How do you know?"

"Marks in the snow," he answered, running his fingers through the air to indicate legs. "From the cabin to some birch about a quarter mile in. And not bear tracks either."

"That wasn't in the report."

"It wouldn't be. I told the dumb suit about it—the federal investigator—but he didn't even bother looking because he said the snow

11

had blown it clear. But I saw them fine. Not a machine, not snowshoes. Not boots."

"Then what?"

He smiled and showed her the half dozen stumps of his teeth. "The closest thing? What I told the dumb suit? A horse."

"A horse," Lily repeated. It wasn't a question. It was to hear from her own mouth something at once impossible and deeply known.

"The suits never put that in any of the write-ups. 'To avoid embarrassment.' Mine, I guess," the old man said. "Because there's no wild horses in Alaska. And no kept horse could have made it through snow that deep even if one had been hauled up that far. It couldn't have gotten *in,* which means it couldn't have gotten *out.*"

It left the question of what happened to be answered by a hypothesis supported by a patchwork of forensics and animal behavior testimony. Lily had been of little help. Deemed unreliable given her age, and traumatized by the shock of losing her only parent. What made her version of events all the more dismissible was the obvious fantasy she'd created. She'd spoken of the dark outline of a ghoul bent over her mother's form, followed by the appearance of a magical creature that carried her out of the bush on its back. Being a psychiatrist now, Lily knew it to be true: children made things up all the time, not only for pleasure, but sometimes to survive.

Even today she "remembers" things from that night. A handful of details recalled with the clarity of a lived event.

She was awakened by the monster knocking at the door.

She thinks of it as this, as a monster, because she knows it wasn't a bear. Because bears don't knock before entering. Because the one difference between animals and people is that animals don't murder, they hunt.

Because she saw it.

2

No matter the weather, Dr. Lily Dominick walks to work every day. Up Second Avenue from her apartment and across the Robert F. Kennedy Bridge to the broad flats of playing fields and institutional campuses of Randalls Island. From there, the most direct way to the Kirby Forensic Psychiatric Center would be to follow the service road that runs beneath the interstate, but Lily keeps to the river instead, sharing the pathway with only the most serious runners and a handful of bored nannies pushing strollers. It takes a little longer, but she always arrives early. There is nothing in her life to make her late.

On this morning, a blue-domed October

wonder, she stops to take in the island of Manhattan she can't help but see, from this south-facing perspective, as a primary school class picture arranged according to height: the stubby apartment buildings and anonymous housing projects growing into the show-offy towers of Midtown. Yet it's not the view that holds her. She looks across the churning water at the smallest building of them all—right up front, where she was made to stand surrounded by strangers in the classroom pictures of her youth—and tries to assess herself as she might the accused she puts questions to at work.

Why is the cabin with you today?

Because of my dream last night.

The old dream. The one you haven't had in years.

It's been a while, yes.

The dream of riding a white horse through the woods after your mother died?

Not *died*. Killed. And I don't think it was a dream. I don't think it was a horse.

Even now? You still think it actually happened? You still believe in magic?

Lily doesn't have an answer for these last questions. Which makes her like most of her clients. They can tell you what they saw, how they did it, what arguments the voices in their heads made. But whether any of it was real? It's like asking a child if the thing living under their bed is real.

She has a gift for the job. One that goes beyond her exceptional performances on exams and the workaholism that was mistaken for ambition but was in fact the comfort she felt walking the asylum's halls. She finds a music in the shouted obscenities and hellish moans emitted from the cells. And then there are the clients themselves. Mutilators, stalkers, worshippers of their own churches of the occult. Malignant souls that most, including her colleagues, largely regard as beyond understanding. Yet Lily doesn't see them that way. She can enter the burnt forests and rubbled cities of their minds and find the pathway to their intentions, the core of their wants buried under ash and rock.

"Why did you do it?" she asks as the final query in most of her interviews.

"I don't know," the murderer or rapist replies.

"I do," Lily says.

She starts walking again, toward the pale brick walls of the Kirby ahead of her, its plainness and enormity not even trying to hide the madhouse that it is. Most of the people she works with, the social workers and orderlies, regularly call the building ugly, or as one bow-tied district attorney who repeatedly hits on her and she repeatedly denies likes to put it, "the Pandemonium on Hell Gate Circle." Lily couldn't disagree more. It was true that where she worked was the sort of place you never wanted to end up. That's why she thought it architecturally honest for it to appear that way. It looked like hell for a reason.

There were so many other positions Lily could have pursued, cushy appointments where she'd refer violent offenders to public institutions like the Kirby but wouldn't have to deal with them directly. Safe and sound. But that was never what she was looking for. It was satisfying to find something you had an affinity for in a university lecture hall, but once she arrived at the Kirby she found it electrifying to practice it in the field. Lily had a special talent for hearing echoes of the demonic voices in the thoughts of her clients, a kind of empathy that her supervisor, Dr. Edmundston, believed marked her for even greater success than she'd already enjoyed in her first few years out, though he admitted that it frightened him a little sometimes. It frightened Lily a little sometimes too. But although the Kirby represented the grimiest corner of psychiatric work, Lily found everything she needed in it. She took home more than enough money for a single woman in a less-than-great apartment who doesn't go out much. And she had never wanted the work to be safe.

You couldn't admit to it, it was unprofessional, it was wrong, but Lily finds stimulation, something almost like arousal, in glimpsing the most diseased minds. It's like looking over the edge of a cliff. If you get close enough, you can feel what it would be like to take one more step and have the world slip out from under you.

A runner rushes toward her.

One of the gaunt marathoners who circle the city's edges day and night. Usually they pass without noticing she's there. But this one, a woman with dark hair tied into a braid that lashes against one shoulder and then the other with each stride, looks directly at her.

There were only a couple of photos ever taken as far as she knew, waxy squares issued from the lips of Polaroid cameras. Pictures of a woman she would compare her own likeness to and sometimes see herself, sometimes not. But as the running woman glances back as she passes, Lily recognizes her.

The running woman looks exactly like her mother.

3

What are you? Some kind of psycho?
Dr. Lily Dominick punches in her security code at the staff entrance as she mentally edits the indictment that has ticker-taped through her mind.

What are you? Some kind—
Some kind of what?
How would the assistant director of Forensic

Psychiatry at one of the leading maximum security institutions of its kind diagnose herself? She knows where to start, anyway. Symptoms. First, a dream from the night before involving her rescue on the back of a white beast. This morning, the memory of a monster as it stood in a pool of blood on the threshold of the cabin's door. And just now, the hallucination of her mother in the face of a stranger.

She can't do it. It's impossible for Lily to see herself as a client because there's no question in her mind that she is fundamentally sane. Given to anxiety in social situations, emotionally more reserved than she ought to be, functionally asexual for longer stretches than she'd like to dwell on, but clinically normal. These visions are only indicative of her imaginative character, she tells herself, not a disorder in the pages of her bible, *Forensic Mental Health Assessment*, Second Edition.

It isn't me, Lily thinks as the door buzzes open and she steps inside the Kirby's walls. *Something in the world has changed today.*

Something that's here. Inside.

She squeaks down the marble floor in the leather flats she traded her sneakers for in a bathroom stall. Choosing comfort over the additional inch or two that heels might afford her, Lily stands five foot four with her back straight. She's little not just in terms of height but proportionally: the slender fingers, the narrow hips, the elven ears. All her life she's been described as *petite,* a word she's come to hate the whole French language for. Yet she's aware of making choices that play up to a certain version of the part. The crisply tailored suits, round tortoiseshell glasses, pageboy haircut. She is at once compact and severe, the sort of woman who men and other women alike tend to call "intense." But there was something enticing in her brand of intensity, something many others saw even if she was blind to it herself. If not an invitation, she offered the promise of a remarkable discovery, a surprising gift to be shared if you could find the key that unlocked her.

As she nods good morning to passing coworkers she gets into the elevator that will take her to her office, all the while telling the second voice within her to be quiet. The voice belongs to her, but is distinct from her own. It's that nasty inner devil all of us have—so Lily believes, a sentimental Freudian at heart—that requires regular taming. *Inappropriate.* You'd never guess it was there, this other voice, coming from this other part of her, manic and grinning within her.

Lily pulls open the door to the cramped anteroom where her assistant Denise's desk is surrounded by towering filing cabinets and a sad chair with a crater in the seat. One look tells Lily that Denise has news. That expression of hers that announces there's something especially juicy to be shared. Her brows raised and her filigreed earrings swinging from recently shaking her head in disbelief.

"Do me a favor and stand here a second," she says as she hands Lily a case file. "I want to see your face when you read what this one did."

"Can't we even try to say good morning first?"

"You're the one who's going to have the good morning. Go on, read it."

"You know these files are confidential, right?"

"I can keep a secret." Denise zips her lips shut.

Lily looks down at the file and sees there's no name on the identification label on the front, only a number. It's not uncommon for clients to show up without knowing who they are, or without telling the police if they do. But this file feels different. A vibrating warmth that travels through the stiff paper and into her fingertips.

"What did he do?" Lily asks.

Denise gets up from her chair to whisper. "Tell you the truth, I don't want to say."

"Why not?"

"Because it's so . . . freaky."

"And you're surprised? Look around. We're in the freak industry."

It's out before Lily can catch herself. *The freak*

industry? The sort of thing Denise says and Lily voices her disapproval of. But this morning it's her line.

"You got that right," Denise says.

4

The man is waiting for her. The file has little to say about him other than his namelessness, the violent crime he was arrested for, his strange calm upon his arrest. He sits at the steel table, palms resting on his knees. In his mug shot, his even gaze was suggestive of considerations that couldn't be guessed at. Now, three strides away, he looks at her and she has even less of an idea what his thoughts may be, even as she can feel him reaching into her head to find hers.

Psycho.

There were so many words you weren't supposed to use that her second voice loved to whisper in her ear. *Psycho,* for one. You never called them that. Over the few years of her still relatively new career she'd watched the patients—no, that had changed too, now they were *clients*—and the words ascribed to them come and go as if borne upon a tide. *Bipolar* for what was once insane, *high-risk* for dangerous. But the truth is—the unspeakable truth, for someone in Dr. Lily Dominick's position—is that the ones who come through the Kirby are all psychos, all dangerous in their ways.

This one the same as the rest.

Lily pulls the security door shut behind her and leaves her hand gripped to the handle a moment longer than necessary to avoid meeting his eyes.

Freaky.

You have to be prepared around people like this, even with their legs shackled to the table that's screwed to the floor. They can be as tricky with the things they say as with the things they do. But this one—a number on a file ten seconds ago and now real—is a man who has done an awful thing and meets her eyes the moment she raises them, conveying something at once brutal and serene. Their shared gaze is weirdly intimate, the kind of look she imagines passes between lovers. It's part of what makes this one different from the others. Which is what likely makes him dangerous, even more so than the other psychos she finds chained to the tables in these rooms that both smell like and are painted the color of boiled peas.

Lily reminds herself of the job she's here to do. This always helps. Once she's in the room, she makes her own feelings disappear. There's only the questions she asks and how they answer them.

This is what drew her to forensic psychiatry in the first place: Lily doesn't treat her clients, she assesses them. There's no obligation to prescribe or heal, merely to categorize, arrive at a conclusion as to their capacity to do the terrible thing they've been accused of, along with their capacity to recognize it as terrible or not. She puts her queries to them and they offer a reply, or hold their silence, or spit yellow bile across the stainless steel table deep within a building more prison than hospital. Sometimes the spit finds her skin.

She releases the door's handle, takes a step into the room, and sees for the second time that it may not be so easy this morning.

The man sitting at the table, half-smiling at her, *is* different from the rest. How can she tell? It isn't his face or his body. Both are pleasing, however unconventionally. The lean strength and broad chest of a swimmer, a power Lily can see even in the interlocked fingers of his large hands. His cheeks and jawline and chin all defined, the skin taut against bone. She guesses he was born in a foreign country, but can't think of any one place his features might belong to.

What truly sets him apart are his eyes. Wide and deep, alive with animal cunning. Gray irises almost swallowed whole by black pupils. Eyes that speak of multiple thoughts happening at once, though they remain outwardly soft, twinkling at some shared humor. The eyes don't make him better or worse than the others, or even

23

necessarily sane. Certainly not innocent. Just different.

"What name have they given me?"

An unplaceable accent. Lily tries to line it up with a culture, a continent, but it sounds to her like a combination of locations and classes. There's Eastern European at its foundation, then a worker's Russian, along with a trace of northeastern American, the Ivy League debate club interpretation of Oxford English. She does all this puzzling over a half dozen words.

He clears his throat. Lily hasn't answered him. She won't say anything until he speaks again.

"Your papers," he says, nodding at the file tucked under her arm. "I'm curious. How do you refer to those who have no names in this place?"

"We assign them a temporary number. Until we discover the client's identity."

"What if you don't?"

"Everyone has a name."

"You are mistaken, Doctor."

He reminds her of a professor she had in grad school. The way he would quiz her, nudge her toward new conclusions. In the case of the professor she'd realized, too late, that it was a subtle form of flirtation. With this man she's sure it isn't about that. Then again, she'd been sure it wasn't about that with the professor too.

"You had no identification with you when you were arrested," she says. "And you've refused to assist investigators by saying who you are. That doesn't make you nameless, though."

The man smiles. A single shift in his expression that makes Lily feel—what? Overwhelmed. Light-headed and heart-tripping in a way that starts out as a response to charm but quickly turns queasily unpleasant, the first lurch of motion sickness.

"Perhaps you will help me," he says.

"Help you?"

"You are a physician, aren't you?"

"Yes."

"That comes with professional obligations toward those like me."

"Like you?"

"The accused." He shrugs and his shoulders make a sound like smoothed bedsheets inside his shirt. "The wicked."

"How would you describe your illness?"

"I said *wicked,* not *ill*."

"Your wickedness then."

"I've grown too accustomed to it to describe it."

"So you see it as my job to tell you?"

"No. I wish your aid in another matter altogether."

"What would that be?"

He smiles again. And again she feels overwhelmed in the same powerfully disorienting way as before.

"Perhaps you could resolve the question of my missing name," he says.

It's playful. A teasing invitation to a harmless game. But there is a commanding authority behind his words too. Soft, gentle, yet it comes to Lily as an order. His voice so persuasive it's almost physical.

Lily closes her eyes. Opens them.

It clears his spell away. Not that she thinks this man is magic or anything like that. *Spell* is just the only word she can think of.

"Can we talk about what brought you here?" she asks.

"Of course." He laughs in a smoker's growl. "But it's a little strange to speak to you like this."

"Like what?"

He gestures at the empty chair across the table from him. "You standing and me sitting. It is, among other things, a situation I find ungentlemanly." He shakes his legs and the shackles around his ankles rattle and clank. "I would rise but my constraints prevent it."

"Yes. I'll sit then," Lily says, but doesn't move. *Ungentlemanly.*

The word holds her. She'd bet it's never been uttered in this room before. She would otherwise expect it to have the ring of sarcasm, given where they are, given the trouble he's in, but it's clear he's serious. A *gentleman*. It's how he regards himself, how he wishes her to see him.

This alone would make him an interesting case if there weren't a dozen other swirling observations in her head that have already made him so.

"I'll sit," she repeats, and this time she does.

She opens his file. He looks at her. She's so aware of him the print swims on the pages.

Pull your shit together, her second voice tells her. *You're acting crazier than he is.*

Control. Lily regards it as her greatest talent. There have been men in this room with her who've told her how they would kill her, confessed to unspeakable acts between bouts of giggles, said things so vile they made her want to take a shower as soon as she left. One or two of these men might have fascinated her for a time until she finally found the slot they deserved in one of the diagnostic textbooks and she realized her fascination was only the passing fizz of professional challenge. Through it all, for every doomed one of them, she'd maintained control.

But now, with this man, she feels something else altogether. Not frightened exactly, but the rush that came with being around someone capable of unpredictable violence. She can tell already that he's intelligent, that she'll have to be ready for curveballs. Yet her excitement isn't of the kind that comes with raising your game in the presence of a worthy opponent. It's the idea that this moment bears meaning for her in ways she couldn't possibly understand now but may come to know if she proves deserving. Along with the unshakeable sense that he's come here for her. Lily feels as if he has delivered a compliment just by sitting there, a prisoner, staring at her.

Stop this. Pull it together. Now.

"You understand the charge against you?" she asks.

"I understand it, yes."

"Assault in the first degree. That's a Class B felony."

" 'A person is guilty of assault in the first degree when, with intent to disfigure another person seriously and permanently, or to destroy, amputate, or disable permanently a member or organ of his body, he causes such injury to such person or to a third person.' I believe that is the relevant subsection."

"You've memorized the criminal code?"

"Not the whole thing. It lacks poetry, wouldn't you say? But I asked to see their book and they let me read it."

"Yes."

"Yes what?"

"I would agree that that's the relevant sub-section. 'Intent to disfigure another person seriously and permanently.' "

He wrinkles his nose and the word *cute* blinks through Lily's mind. *Sexy,* her inappropriate voice corrects. *Not cute. But most definitely sexy.*

"I might contest the 'permanently,' " he says.

"They can do such wonderful things with plastic surgery nowadays."

She considers writing *Narcissistic personality disorder? => lack of compassion; primary injury inflicted to appearance, not victim's body* in her notes but doesn't want to break the flow of words between them.

"Could you tell me what happened?" she asks.

"I tore a man's ears from his head."

"There was no knife?"

"It didn't require a knife."

"That's unusual."

"Is it?"

He blinks. So slow, the room so quiet that she can hear it.

"Ripping ears off with your bare hands," she says. "Yes, I'd say unusual. How did you do it?"

He shows his hands. Brings both forefingers together with the thumbs to make a pair of rings. "I took them like this, and pulled, like this." He brings his hands down and the cuffs around his wrists clang off the table's edge.

"That's all it took?"

"The human body is more pliant than most seem to think. More fragile too."

"Did you approach the man from behind?"

"No. He was walking one way and I the other."

"He didn't resist?"

"How can you resist what you have no reason to anticipate?"

"Did you speak to him?"

"Yes."

"What did you say?"

"Breathe in."

"Why that?"

"Because I knew he would do as I told him. And that by the time he breathed out I'd be done."

Once more Lily has to return her eyes to the file pages on the table, using them as an anchor to the world outside the room.

"I've seen the photos," she says, flipping the pages with her thumb. "With hands alone—I wouldn't think it possible."

"Normally, no. I suppose not." The man nods as if at an unexpected consideration.

"And you're not normal."

"Not remotely."

"So tell me," she says, looking up at him again. "Share your ear-tearing secret with me."

He ignores her playfulness as easily as she succumbed to his.

"It demands a certain amount of strength, certainly," he answers. "And the absence of hesitation. That above all."

"You felt no hesitation because the man deserved what you did to him?"

"No, no. You misunderstand." She's reminded

once again of her grad school professor, this time of his impatience. "It's that I feel no hesitation about *any* action I take."

She makes a note in the file. A scribbled shorthand. He watches her write and Lily is sure they both see the meaninglessness of what she does.

"You think a statement like that brings you closer to finding a condition for me," he says. "Something in the sociopathic family, I'd imagine."

"It's an interesting aspect. That's all. But I'd like to know more."

"I'm here for you, Doctor."

He tries to spread his arms wide in a gesture of openness but the restraints prevent him, so that he merely raises his hands clasped together in front of his face as if in prayer.

When he lowers them she considers his face without looking away.

You'd never mistake him for a pretty man, nor perhaps even handsome, but he's unquestionably appealing. The long, flared nose, the scrubby islands of beard, the eyes downturned at the corners so that they convey a constant expression of what could be either empathy or gnawing grief. There are indications of strength in even the smallest of his motions. Not bulging, weight-lifted muscle, but sinewy, like braided rope. She was wrong in her initial impression of him as a swimmer. There's an elegance to that sport—the progress of an individual body against a resisting element—he would have little interest in. Lily's client has the physical presence of someone who has never done anything in pursuit of athletics, rather only to bring about immediate alterations to his environment, the delivery of pleasure or the infliction of pain. His nature strikes her as equal parts lover and street fighter.

It's the mouth. The other parts too, but Lily thinks it's the mouth above all. Full and sharply etched. A mouth to kiss, to open yourself to. "I'm no expert," Lily always says whenever Denise hands her a photo of some movie star in one of the magazines she brings to work and asks if Lily thinks he's hot. "Good-looking, I guess, but I'm no expert." As if expertise were required to respond to the way someone looks.

"Why did you decide to hurt him, a stranger?" she asks, looking down at the file again.

"Proximity."

"To what?"

"The police cruiser parked on West Broadway."

"You wanted to be seen?"

"Yes."

"To be arrested?"

"Yes."

"Why his ears?"

"I needed to do something out of the ordinary."

"Why?"

"Aren't those the kind they send you? The scary ones?"

"So you did this because you want to be locked up in a forensic psychiatric facility?"

"Not at all, Doctor. I did this because I want to be with you."

Lily leans back in her chair. The man hasn't made any move toward her but she catches a scent of his skin as if he'd placed his hands on her cheeks. There's woodsmoke in it, and some kind of grain alcohol. The sawdust and aged meat of the butcher shop.

"You think you know who I am?" she asks, and immediately sees it's the wrong question. If a client believes a relationship exists between himself and his examiner, it's important to point out that this connection is a side effect of their deviance, a false illusion of intimacy. A physician in her position has to either get things back on track or end the interview altogether and try again another time. Lily has made a mistake. She's given this man the opportunity to confirm his convictions. Which he does.

"Of course I know you," he says.

"So tell me."

"You are Dr. Lily Dominick. Thirty-six years old. Unmarried, no children. You completed your residency in forensic psychiatry at Brown, and prior to that graduated summa cum laude in biological science at the University of Michigan.

33

All on full scholarship, give or take a part-time job here and there. The Kirby has been your sole place of employment since entering practice, which I can assume is because you chose it to be. You wanted nothing but the best. Which, in your field, means nothing but the worst."

"My name. That's all you're working from," Lily replies, speaking with intentional force to cover the tremble in her voice. "It's public knowledge who's on staff here. My CV is on the web somewhere too, along with my birth date for all I know. A diligent Internet search. Quite a different thing from knowing me."

"Very true. As it stands, you are little more than a collection of facts to me. But I hope that will soon change."

"It won't."

"Hold on to your doubt, Doctor. It will provide you some comfort for a time."

"Until what?"

"Until it turns to dust. Until your old life ends and your new one begins."

She jots another note. This one to compose the right question, one that will allow her to slip away from his tightening knot of riddles.

"If you really knew me," she says, "you would know the names of my mother and father."

"Clever! You are setting traps for me!"

"How so?"

"Because you never had a father, at least one

you ever knew. And your mother—what is the polite term in America? Not *dead,* certainly not! You're allergic to the idea in this country, even the mention of it. Your mother has *passed on.* But it was she with whom I had an acquaintanceship. Before you were born and up until—"

"—*died.* I'm not offended by the term."

"Of course! What physician would be? *Died.* There! Let's both be grown-ups."

It's only a successful shot in the dark—to guess a single parenthood, no names, no specific circumstances—but Lily has to remind herself of it. He's on a fishing expedition and nothing else. Just like the psychic who chances on the dead loved one whose name starts with a vowel ("Uncle Ed!") and is credited with uncanny accuracy, this man is feeling around until she helps him find a nugget of particularity. Something she's not about to do. First, because it's her job to turn this interview around. Second, she doesn't like the idea that he possesses even a piece of faked knowledge of her past.

"There are a number of problems with your proposition," Lily states calmly.

"Yes?"

"For one, it would appear that we're about the same age. Which means if I was a child when you knew my mother, you were a child too. Even if you had met her—which I don't believe—you wouldn't have remembered it, given how young you would have been."

"You said a number of problems. Could you cite another?"

"You haven't given my mother a name, or stated where you knew her from."

There's a clock on the wall and the man glances up at it, rightly calculating that these interviews have fixed time limits. His shackles clank together under the table as he weighs what approach he should take.

"I have many things I'd like to say that you will find unbelievable at first. Specifics are where that doubt of yours puts me at a disadvantage, especially here, where I can't show you things, only speak them," he says. "Yet I look forward to our future discussions, Doctor. They will require some time. That's where the showing will be of assistance."

"I can observe more than you think from right here," Lily says, placing her elbows on the table. "And my hearing is fine. It's my job to listen."

"Then hear this. I am not like anyone who has ever passed through this place before. I am a singular case."

"Were you trying to prove your singularity when you injured that man the way you did?"

He takes a deep breath. "Let's stop talking about him."

"Isn't he the reason we're together right now?"

"No. He means nothing."

"The pain you caused him. Are you saying—"

"No!"

The man stands. Kicks at the leg shackles with such force the table, the floor itself shakes. His hands clenched in fists he stops himself from swinging down. Lily flinches, but almost instantly sits straight again.

"I'm not here to explain a petty crime! I'm not a *case study!* I thought you—"

He stops once he realizes he's shouting. He sits. His eyes dart to the door to see if an officer will appear. Lily half expects it herself. But whether the guard on the other side of the glass is too busy dunking his donut or whether he's waiting for a signal she has yet to give, the door remains closed.

"I'm here to give you a gift," the man says, his voice no more than a whisper.

Lily closes the file. "I should go."

"Please don't."

"These interviews—they can't happen if—"

"I promise I won't do that again. I will be patient. And it's really the most extraordinary gift. Please, Lily."

The way he says her name. It sounds to her, with that accent of his, closer to its true articulation than when she says it herself. She lingers, partly to confirm her diagnosis by learning what he wants to present her with, partly to hear him say her name again.

"What gift?" she asks.

"Something I've never wholly shared with anyone before."

"A secret."

"If it's a secret, it's been sitting right under mankind's nose for a very long time."

"It's special knowledge, then."

"Only the truth, Doctor."

Lily puts her pen down. Gestures for him to continue.

"It's true by appearance we would seem to belong to the same generation," he begins. "Which would mean I was a child at the same time you were. But the fact is I was never a child."

"Metaphorically, I take it."

"Not at all."

"I don't follow."

"I came into the world in this adult form, and have remained this way all my life. A life that's over two hundred years old, Dr. Dominick."

Lily nods as casually as she can and picks up her pen. Makes another note in the file.

Irrational age claim. Constancy = appearance. Supernatural attributes.

It's almost disappointing. Even this one, so interesting, so seemingly different, is falling into place, into a category.

Delusions of immortality consistent
with schizophrenia => indication
of Cotard's Syndrome?

He was going in this direction all along, she recognizes now. It was his intensity—his seasick-making attractiveness—that put her off course at first. But now he's coming into diagnostic focus just like all the others. Which makes this day just like all the ones that came before. It makes her feel old. Two hundred years old.

"The longest recorded life span of a human being is one hundred and twenty years," she says. "You're aware of this?"

"One hundred and twenty-two years and one hundred and sixty-four days. Yes, I'm aware of it."

"So you see yourself as an exception?"

"Yes."

"How?"

"In the simplest terms? I'm not a human being."

Ah, here we go, Lily thinks. Which will it be? Alien or angel? It's usually one of those two. Though she's prepared to give this one the credit of coming up with something a little more original.

"You beg the question, 46874-A," Lily says, reading the number on the stickered ID of his file. "If not human, what are you?"

He smiles. But it's not like his earlier ones. There's sadness in his face now that transfers to her, an instant, swelling despair in her chest.

"I think the answer to that is why I'm here," he says.

"You've said that already. To have someone give you a name."

"No, Lily." His face drifts closer to hers over the table, a distance greater than she would have guessed his leg shackles would allow. "To have you know what I am."

It comes to her all at once. The fear.

He'd made her alert from the moment she'd entered the room. But she hadn't felt truly frightened until now.

To have you know what I am.

The layers of unwanted discovery he implies with this sentence alone, a darkness that goes deeper than any psychiatric condition—it enters her like a bullet of ice to the chest.

"I have another appointment," she mumbles as she sweeps the file up and stands. "We'll have to arrange—"

She knocks her chair back without meaning to and it clatters to the floor. This seems to get the guard's attention, because she hears the buzzer that opens the door. Only ten feet away but looking three times that distance now. She doesn't stop to right the chair. She doesn't look back at him.

"Alison," the shackled man says.

"What did you say?"

"She went by other names at different times in her life, but that's most likely what you knew her as."

Lily can't find words. Or air. She makes it to the door but goes still once she gets there, her hand riveted to the handle.

"Your mother," he says. "I knew her, Lily. In ways you didn't. Still don't."

"How did you—"

"Your mother was not who she presented herself as. Not at all."

"That's not—"

"She told you a story. And as you grew up in other people's homes, you passed it along until you could construct your own story. But I have come here to tell you that what you know of your origins contains only the smallest fragment of truth."

It takes all her will to do it, but Lily turns to face him. "Why don't you tell me. Tell me the truth."

"Your father wasn't a man named Jonathan. Those few photos of him that you possess are pictures of a stranger that your mother gave you so that it would appear you were the product of a brief coupling, that they had gone their separate ways."

"That's enough."

"While the woman you know as Alison was your mother—"

"Shut *up!*"

"While Alison was your mother, the man in those photos—Jonathan—played no part in your conception."

"You're wrong," she says. "Jonathan Dominick was my father."

"No, he wasn't."

"How do you know?"

"Because I am."

5

Lily staggers from the interview room with her hands held out at her sides, partly to brace herself, partly to fend off any attack. The latter concerns her more than the dizziness that feels like a nest of birds trapped in her head, beating their wings against the inside of her skull. Defend herself? From what? The client was being taken to his cell by way of a separate, secured hallway. He is no threat now. But it doesn't stop her from feeling threatened. The half-smile and swallowing eyes of the man in chains. *She told you a story.* Her mother's body. The thing standing over it.

She can feel the nameless client inside the building. Somewhere in the concrete vastness of the Kirby's long halls he radiates a heat that makes her look behind her more than once over the course of the day to check if he's standing there. Each time there's a second of real surprise when he isn't.

Lily knows this is only her returning to what he said, over and over. Odd in itself. Clients said bizarre things to her all the time and, for the most part, none of it echoed in her head once she'd shut the interview room door. She tries to tell herself it's because what the man said was so personal. But then again, clients had tried to get under her skin before, tried to make it about her. None of them could back it up with obscure facts the way the man from this morning had. Is that why his voice lingers? The psych studies say it's the same way with ghosts. The dead appear most vividly to those already looking for them, so that those suffering grief see the one grieved for just as those playing with a Ouija board unknowingly move the planchette with their own fingers. A series of links of her own making: she's thinking of him, and this gives her the sensation of his presence, so that it seems he's reaching out to her just as she is to him.

Hold on to your doubt, Doctor.

He needn't have bothered telling Lily that. Doubt is the one part of herself she doesn't have to worry about losing. Her clients' talk is little more than a patchwork of scenarios, guesses, denials, delusions. She mistrusts people for a living. It's also why she worked so hard at school, now that she thinks of it. Those glowing report cards, the scholarships, the letter of acceptance from the Kirby—she'd been suspicious of all of them. She knows where talk therapy would ultimately lead her on this issue. Her mother. The way she died. A child who believed it was a monster who knocked at the cabin door. A white Pegasus flying through the forest with her on its back.

No, she had never had a problem with doubt.

She can pull apart the things he said to her all too easily—her parents' names would have required a little digging, but any obsessive with a computer and time on his hands could've gotten that far. The rest of it even more easily dismissed. Over two hundred years old. Never aging in appearance. The claim about being her father. You didn't need an advanced psychiatric degree to write all of it off as batshit crazy.

So why are you looking over your shoulder every five minutes?

He's different.

She'd felt it from the moment she'd seen him. Even before that, on her walk to work that morning, seeing a woman with her mother's face run by. And before that too. The dream of the monster.

There is no link between these moments and

dreams and yet her mind travels between them with the fluency of coherence. Her mother, the man in the interview room, the thing in the cabin. Back to her mother again.

Lily remembers her in detail in some respects, and not at all in others. It was like viewing a landscape from five thousand feet. Sometimes the clouds cover everything in gray, and sometimes they pull away to show the smoke rising from a chimney, the swing set in the yard, a figure clipping laundry to a line.

One of the details that reveals itself now is how, before the lullabies that sent her off to sleep, there were often bedtime stories too. Lily suspects they must have been made up on the spot, as none of the plots correspond to any children's classics she's aware of, no Dr. Seuss rhymes or talking animals or books with charming pictures in them. In fact, they didn't seem like stories you'd ever tell a kid her age. They were too frightening, for one thing. A man who went into a forbidden room and was almost devoured by women who turned into fiends. A boy who stayed out too late at night who was kicked and kicked by a stranger in the street until his head broke open. A doctor who discovered a way of putting a ghost into a graveyard corpse. The grown-up Lily had always considered them homemade variations on the Brothers Grimm, their intent to caution and instruct. But now she sees her mother's tales as worse than that, sicker than that. They were horror stories.

Lily flips through the catalogue of her memory to find a warmer, more wholesome clip, so that when her mother's hair comes to mind she holds on to it. A kind of dark that was almost liquid in the way it bent light into stripes down its length. Lily would snuggle against her mother's back and shroud her face with hair, peering through it like a waterfall. Now the scent of it returns to her. A vanilla that had nothing to do with any shampoo or conditioner but came from her mother's skin, the essence of her that clung to the soft black strands.

Lily's hair would be just like it if she didn't cut it to her jawline. She always assumed this was to assert a no-nonsense, professional demeanor but realizes now it may have as much to do with avoiding the pain of seeing her mother in the mirror every time she looked if she allowed it to grow.

Now a new question: If she felt her mother so keenly through the distance of the past, why did her father—his image, his name—return nothing specific to her? The man in the room was right in this at least: Jonathan Dominick had only ever registered to her as the photo of a stranger. Which is not to say the idea of a father was without life for her. She felt his absence acutely, as acutely as the revulsion at her mother's murder, a space like an insatiable gnawing in her heart.

You want your daddy, her voice says. *It's so like you to feel the most for the thing that was never there.*

Then another voice. His.

Until your old life ends and your new one begins.

Despite all her doubt, it seems to Lily it already has.

A new life. More vivid than the one before today, the whole of her body prickly and alive. She couldn't say she's happier (measuring happiness has never been easy for her, like looking down into a dark lake and guessing the distance to its muddy bottom), yet there's a skin that's been peeled away from her today all the same. It's left her weightless. Going through the tasks of her agenda—the lunch meeting with a colleague that boiled down to complaints about inadequate air-conditioning in his office, the returning of inconsequential e-mails. It took more than a little self-control to not tell her colleague to buy his own damn air conditioner if he didn't like the "incessant rattling" from the one the hospital gave him. Even replying to a request for advice on a file from Dr. Edmundston, the kindly man who hired her and whom she adored, felt like a chore.

Whatever shape this new life ended up taking, it's clear to Lily that her inappropriate voice was going to have a bigger say in things.

• • •

She's so distracted by the morning's interview that Lily almost forgets she has a date tonight.

"So," her assistant says, tapping a pen against her lower lip. "What are you going to wear?"

"Wear?"

Denise drops the pen. Snaps her fingers. "Calling Dr. Dominick. Hel-*lo?*"

"Sorry. I'm a little lost today."

"I'm asking how you're going to look for your man."

Your man.

For a second, Lily thinks Denise is talking about her client from this morning.

That's when she remembers the guy from the dating website. A name and photo and profile that accepted her name and photo and profile and now these two avatars are going to meet at a restaurant. It was Denise who'd talked her into it. She explained to Lily how people didn't *meet* anymore, didn't *date,* they *hooked up.*

"You don't want to be alone forever, do you?" she'd asked.

At the time, the part that made Lily feel even older than being coached at romance by a woman only three years younger than herself was that maybe the answer was yes, she did want to be alone forever.

She recalls how she found the man she's to meet

for dinner nice-looking when she'd accepted his invitation. *Hot.* Denise's word. Now hers.

Lily checks her watch. Three forty-two. She tallies what work remains before her for the day: two more client interviews and a stack of notes to be dictated, then an important Scheduling Committee meeting, Dr. Edmundston sitting as Chair.

"Cancel the rest of my day," Lily says, grabbing her coat.

"What? What'll I say?"

"Say I'm sick."

"But where are you going?"

"Shopping."

Lily's clothes are expensive. The only aspect of herself she splurges on. Tailored blouses and jackets and pants, a Midtown uniform of top-tier feminine professionalism. But there is little in her wardrobe that would qualify as sexy. The simple fact is she doesn't really think about sex anymore, let alone have much of it. How long has it been? She's startled to realize it's a stretch measurable in years, not months. She had a ready-made loop of excuses for the increasingly rare occasions when she worried it might indicate a larger problem: the difficulty of finding a decent guy in New York, the demands of work, the preference of a glass of wine and Netflix at the end of the day over conversation. Honesty would require her to add another reason. She's lost touch with desire.

You've lost touch with your body, her inner voice clarifies. *As in, nobody's been touching it. Not even you.*

Yet here she is, trying on clothes that reveal her curves instead of the tidy lines she'd grown used to. Clothes she could never wear to the Kirby. *Sexy.* This is the word she uses after skipping off work for the first time since getting the job, taking a cab to Midtown, and strolling down Fifth Avenue.

"I'm looking for something sexy," she tells the first salesperson in every door she enters.

It isn't easy.

Lily is striking—big almond eyes, delicate mouth, a dancer's body—but she's always chosen good taste over boldness. It's an approach that extends to more than just her clothes. "A tamer and shamer," as her professor-lover had called her. He'd meant it approvingly, as he was the kind of man who liked to imagine he deserved discipline, and needed someone to remind him how bad he was. But the remark had wounded Lily. Not as an indicator of how she treated her boyfriends, but how she treated herself. Taming and shaming. Enough truth in it to hurt.

Was there an option? She was a doctor, a professional. A woman. *Petite.* For someone in her position, it's what you had to do. Stay controlled, let your balance earn you the authority that comes automatically to others, to men. Lily's inner voice liked to remind her of what she would be capable if she let all of it go. There was power in the opposite of balance. Her clients showed her every day. The things that impulse could achieve, the liberty of recklessness. Madness. For as long as she could remember she'd never allowed even a taste of it to enter her bloodstream.

Today she would make an exception.

As she tries on a cocktail dress the saleswoman describes as "deadly," her phone vibrates in her purse. Another e-mail from Dr. Edmundston, asking if she's okay. *Please remember, Lily. You can talk to me.* And it's true. He's as close to a mentor, to a father, as she's ever had.

She can't outright lie to the man. But the truth won't do either. So she goes with something between the two.

Lionel—
I'm fine. Just a queasy stomach
(beware the cafeteria salad bar!).
Apologies for missing the meeting.
Will call in the morning.
Thanks for your concern,
L

In the mirror, as she turns to see how the dress sculpts her body, she pretends the man from the interview room is watching her. She wonders if he'd like what he saw. What part of her his eyes would settle on. Where he'd reach out to touch first.

"I'll take this one," she says.

Her date doesn't look quite as good as he did in his photos. Lily guesses this is standard. And he's not as interesting as she'd expected him to be from the profile—mountain climber, working "private equity plays" on solar energy farms—but he's good-looking enough, interesting enough. Lily can't help but compare him to the man from the interview room this morning and find him something less.

What the hell is wrong with you? That was a client. A psycho. This is a date.

It's an ongoing struggle to remember the name of the man sipping the wine and forking the halibut across the table from her. To remind herself, she slips it into the conversation as often as she can.

"But Tim, aren't you ever afraid when you look down from the summit?"

"Can I ask you something personal, Tim?"

"I'd like to go now, Tim."

This last one before their desserts arrive.

"Are you feeling all right?" he asks, pushing his seat back as if in readiness to perform the Heimlich on her.

"I'd really like to go to your apartment," she says. It's a surprise, even to herself.

He's surprised too. But not so surprised that he doesn't stand and make a signature-signing gesture for the waiter to bring the check.

Even during sex she makes sure to call him Tim.

It's to try to stop imagining that it's not her online date who's in bed with her but today's client. Because she can't keep thinking of him as this—*her client*—and 46874-A doesn't work either, she gives him a name. Thinks of him as Ivan.

Don't let him into your thoughts, Lily. Especially now. Stay with this man. With Tim.

What would he be like? Not the solar energy guy, but Ivan. Here, in bed?

She's sure he wouldn't be like this.

Though this is really good—Tim is nothing if not attentive, eager to show her his trademark tricks, his smooth shifts of position—in Lily's mind it's all lovemaking. Ivan would be less aware of their presumed roles, less self-congratulatory in his generosity.

It's that I feel no hesitation in any action I take.

Ivan would fuck her.

Tim is still asleep when Lily awakens to the sound of crickets.

The clock radio on the bedside table reads

53

2:42 A.M. The crickets are her phone's signal of an incoming call. Aside from Denise using it to pull her out of interviews that have gone overtime, or her yoga instructor notifying her of a canceled class, nobody calls her.

She slips out of bed and carries her purse into the bathroom down the hall. Closes the door.

"Hello?"

"Lily? It's Dr. Edmundston."

"Lionel. I'm so sorry. I didn't want you to be worried—"

"This isn't about you missing yesterday's meeting. It's rather more urgent than that."

Edmundston's voice is calm, even though he's calling her at a quarter to three. But Lily's heard that version of calmness before. She uses it herself with some of her less predictable clients.

"What is it?" Lily asks. "What's wrong?"

"I can't talk about it over the phone. Could you come to my apartment?"

"Now?"

"If you're feeling well enough. If it's not too much trouble."

"I don't understand. Why can't—"

"This all sounds strange, I know. But you're the only one I can speak to about this. Please. Would you come?"

"Of course. Just give me time to—"

But Dr. Edmundston had already hung up.

6

She'd been to Dr. Edmundston's apartment several times before, for dinners and departmental gatherings, but never on her own. The possibility that this is some kind of romantic invitation occurs to her, though she immediately dismisses it. Lionel Edmundston is divorced, midfifties, his two kids away at college. Lily gets the impression that his new freedom has given him the chance to pursue a different life. He will sometimes mention going to the opera or movies at the Angelika with "my companion," and she understands this to mean another man.

Lily asks the cab driver to drop her off at the corner of Madison and Ninety-Sixth Street, and she walks the rest of the way to Edmundston's building. It's the hour when even in New York you can find yourself the only one on the block, just as Lily finds herself now. She's unpracticed at the high heels thing so that her new shoes scratch the sidewalk every third step. *Clop-clop-scrawwp.* It strikes her that if she needed to run she could go no faster than she's going now.

She hits the call button for Edmundston's unit and within seconds his voice crackles out of the speaker.

"Lily?"

"It's me."

The door buzzes.

Instead of opening it, she feels the overwhelming urge to turn and *clop-clop-scrawwp* her way back down the street. She doesn't have to do this. If Lionel Edmundston is worried about an interdepartmental civil war, if he's asking her to help him cover up some embarrassing negligence, if he's on the edge of a nervous breakdown—it doesn't have to be her to go up the stairs and knock on his door in the middle of the night.

It's not that, you bullshit artist, her inner voice says. *It's because you're scared.*

The exterior door buzzes and buzzes.

She shoulders it open.

Up the stairs to the second floor. The street outside pulling at her through the walls like a magnet but she fights it off by going as fast as she's able. When she comes to Edmunston's unit she finds the door is ajar. He's saved her from the new round of hesitation that knocking would have brought on. All she has to do is push the door wider and walk in.

She pushes it wider. Walks in.

Lily loves this place. The high ceilings, arched windows, the exposed brick wall. And on the Upper East Side too. She has no idea how Lionel affords it. Family money, probably.

The New Yorker's go-to answer to the puzzling calculations of apartment envy.

It's this distraction that prevents her from immediately noticing the place is mostly dark. The only illumination comes from a single standing lamp at the corner of the sofa. That, and a dim yellow spilling out from behind the kitchen wall, as if he'd left the fridge door open.

"Lionel?"

"Come in," he answers from the kitchen. "Would you like a drink?"

"No, thank you."

Two ice cubes drop into a rock glass and she waits for the gurgle and splash of something poured over them, but if there is, it's too faint to hear.

"Please, close the door and come in, Lily," he says.

Close the door.

Does he sound normal? Is this a normal place to be, a normal thing to be doing?

No, no, and no.

The strangeness of the situation hits her in a way that pulling down the jeans of her date didn't, that collecting her clothes from the floor of his room and leaving without leaving a note behind didn't. It's because she'd chosen those things, and this had chosen her. There had been too many oddities in the last twenty-four hours already. Now, standing in Lionel Edmundston's underlit apartment, she sees that abandoning control eventually leads you to this. You bluff and go all in enough times and your luck is guaranteed to run out.

She's moving backward to the door when Edmundston appears from the kitchen. It's too dark to make out the details of his face. He's holding the glass with the ice cubes.

"Thank you for coming," he says.

He sounds normal, even if the situation isn't.

"I knew if you were calling me at this hour it was important," she says as she steps closer. "But I've got to tell you, this is all a bit—"

His face.

Now that she's only a few feet away from him, the light from the lamp shows what she couldn't see earlier. It's Dr. Edmundston, but he's been crying. A string of spit hanging from his lower lip. His whole body shaking.

Go.

His mouth shapes around this word, but no sound comes out.

Lily tries to move but the weight of her legs has doubled. She could no more run from the room than make herself disappear by snapping her fingers.

A shadow moves across the floor.

Lily watches as a figure emerges from the kitchen to stand behind Edmundston. It places a hand on his shoulder. A hand that's not a hand. The fingers too long, the tips curled and pointed, metallic.

A claw.

The figure leans its head forward as if to whisper something in Edmundston's ear. Far enough to bring half its face into the light.

It's him. The man from the pea-green interview room. The one Lily had started to think of as Ivan. Though she will never think of him as that ever again.

"Don't make a sound," the man says.

It's not clear whether he's addressing Edmundston or her, but both of them remain quiet.

The man's free hand lifts something the size of an apple to his mouth. Is it food he'd pulled from the fridge and has decided he would now finally eat? She waits for the crunching sound of his bite. Instead, he opens his mouth almost impossibly wide and pushes the thing inside. Clicks it into place.

He parts his lips wide.

Teeth.

Silver. Oversized and sharp. The incisors long and thin as needle points.

"Watch," he says.

Edmundston's fingers slip away from the glass he holds and it shatters on the floor, spinning ice cubes and a thousand diamond chips over the hardwood. The man waits for Lily's eyes to return to his, then he sinks his silver teeth into the side of Edmundston's throat.

Lily does as she's told. She watches.

There's very little blood. Where she would expect to see it spilling down the white of Edmundston's neck and soaking through his shirt there's only a moist ring around the man's lips. It takes a moment to understand why.

It's because he's not only biting. He's feeding.

Go!

Lionel had tried to warn her. So afraid that the utterance of this single word was all he was capable of. Now she whispers the same word to herself.

Look away . . . and go!

It makes no difference.

There's nothing stopping Lily from back-stepping out the door. Nothing but him. Held to the spot by the man's command to witness this as surely as if her feet were screwed to the floor like the table in the Kirby's pea-green room.

She tries to concentrate on Lionel, to communicate some reassurance, the comfort that there is a friend here with him. But his eyes only goggle at her, his skin growing paler, turning to paper. His mouth open, gasping. The Adam's apple in his throat lurches up and down as he gulps at spit and air.

It's easier to look at the man.

She hears the broken glass moving over the floor and sees it's from Edmundston's shoes, kicking and pedaling. Making only glancing contact with the floorboards because the man behind him has lifted him up as if he were the weight of a child.

It doesn't take long but it feels like the whole of the night.

The man pulls his teeth out of Edmundston's throat and drops him. Her colleague writhes on the floor, grinding shards of glass into his clothes. But this for only a moment. There's a final spasm, along with a sound that may be an attempt at a word—*beat* or *meat* or *eat*—and then he's still.

The man steps over the body and comes toward Lily.

He will do the same to her.

That's what will happen next. He wanted her to watch so she could know what it was to die in the way he delivered it. Yet his face tells her otherwise. The crimson line around his mouth like misapplied lipstick. An expression of what may be sympathy. The look a father gives his child before taking the old family dog to the vet to be put down.

Before he touches her, he stops. A strange sensation of slowness overcomes her. Time stretched like chewed gum, thinning and thinning but never breaking. She doesn't look away. She can't.

"Sleep," he says.

Then she steps off the cliff and she's falling.

7

Dear Lily,

I know what you're thinking, but don't do it. Don't call the police. Don't tell anyone. I would say you would regret it but you wouldn't live long enough for that.

This adventure—is that the right word? this revelation? this exchange of gifts?— is between you and me. There are so many things I wish you to discover, truly startling things, but I cannot be at your side the whole way. Aside from the police, there are other, far more dangerous elements who pursue me, and if they see you as my accomplice, they will destroy you as swiftly as they seek to destroy me.

Even now, you may feel compelled to involve the authorities. This urge must be resisted.

First, consider how fantastical the truth would sound: an escaped madman lured you to your superior's apartment so that you could witness his—his what? His biting the man's neck with silver teeth? His feeding? Take a moment. Think of uttering these statements to a homicide detective under fluorescent lights and only a styrofoam cup of bitter coffee to calm you.

If your conscience still has you reaching for the phone, let's consider the other factors. The doctor's blood, to begin. In your sleep, I applied some to your hands, your clothes. Touched your fingerprints to the floor, the table, the door handle. Not a concern for someone such as yourself whose DNA would not exist in the current library. But if you came forward the police would run every test they could. It would be a simple matter after that to pin the murder on you.

Have you been inside your kitchen yet? Note the absence of the blade from your block. Of course, you saw me snuff out Dr. Edmundston's life before your eyes. But once I'd put you to sleep I used your knife—taken from your apartment while you were at dinner with your handsome stranger—to add new injuries to the doctor's body. Coroners don't look for custom-fashioned teeth, Lily, they look for the obvious. Those odd puncture marks will be a mystery, to be sure, if brought up at your trial. But your knife? More than sufficient to make you a murderer.

I have the knife. If you do not do as I say, I will mail it to the police.

What am I asking you to do? Only one thing.

Come to me.

I am the escapee, the ear ripper, the killer of a prison guard. A man with no name. They will search for me so long as they don't have anyone else—as long as they don't have you—on their list. They will track me like an animal.

As ever, if I am to be an animal, I will be the superior animal.

If I am to be hunted, it will be the hunters who suffer.

8

Lily awakens on the floor of Dr. Edmundston's apartment and recognizes immediately where she is.

Her first thought is that she was at one of Lionel's dinner parties and had fainted. Too much wine on an empty stomach. A food allergy discovered at an inopportune time. She looks around for the guests to express her embarrassment to, but the apartment is empty. No music. And dark for a party.

Then it all comes back.

It's the color of the lampshade from the room's only light that triggers her memory. The beige-softened bulb that revealed Lionel's face before the man stepped out of the kitchen and placed the hooked claws on his shoulder. The light that allowed her to see the horror in Edmundston's eyes, the knowledge that he was about to die and had delivered her to the same fate for no other reason than the man had asked him to.

But the man hadn't killed Lily. He'd put her to sleep.

Some kind of instant hypnosis that dropped her to the floor and left her dreamless and still for—how long? She checks her purse for her phone to see what time it is but it's gone. Which means she can't call 911. Edmundston, she knows, doesn't have a landline. And she guesses the man took Edmundston's cell just like he'd taken hers. She could check to make sure, but a combination of revulsion and the cautions of her interior voice prevents her.

Everything around you is wet paint. Touch it and you leave a mark behind.

She tries not to, but can't leave without looking at the body. She needs to know. A part of her still clings to the possibility that what she thinks she's recalling is only something she'd dreamed. So she turns once she's on her feet. Edmundston is there, a shrunken, desiccated version of the living man. Then she sees the dark spill of blood around his head and remembers that half of him, the liquid insides, had been stolen by the man with the silver teeth.

When she opens the door onto the street Lily stands there wondering what should be done first. The police should be involved, she knows this. But she's not sure if pay phones exist anymore and instinct tells her it would be a bad decision to stop a stranger or hail a cab.

Go home, her voice tells her. *You'll be able to think there.*

It isn't far. Once she finds Second Avenue she starts walking uptown. Then she pulls the shoes from her feet and runs.

In times of trouble, Lily makes lists. She's still writing one in her head—call police, take one of her pills before hiding them, check e-mail to see if anyone has sent news of how the man got out of the Kirby—when she arrives at her apartment and makes sure all three of her locks are secure once she gets inside.

Later, she'll wonder why it never occurred to her that the man might be inside waiting for her.

It may have been that the door showed no sign of being tampered with, and as she lives on the sixth floor, there is no other way he could have gotten in. It may be the sense that he wouldn't have had the time—though when she passed a clock in a corner store window on her way home it showed 5:42 A.M., which meant she hadn't just fainted, but had been out at least two hours. It may have been that she didn't think the man would come here to kill her when he could have done that at Dr. Edmundston's.

Whichever it was, it made finding the blood on her kitchen counter a surprise.

A snaking smear at the base of her knife block, as if a hand had found something there and pulled casually away, leaving its mark behind. That's when she sees that the block's largest slot is empty. Her knife. The big Henckel she only used to tackle the tough stuff, the plastic packaging and pineapples.

That's where she finds the letter telling her not to go to the police. Hastily written on a memo pad using a bloodstained ballpoint pulled from a kitchen drawer.

Lily rushes to the bathroom to be sick but nothing comes up.

No good would come from looking in the mirror over the sink but she does it anyway. It's a need to know this is really her seeing these things. If this was a particularly convincing nightmare, looking at her reflection would be the moment when she would instead see a goat's head, or her dead mother's face, or the man's—something that would be shocking and horrible but reveal the past hours for the unreal narrative she hoped it was. Instead, she's met by herself. Unfamiliar makeup applied for her date, now smeared from sex and tears. She turns on the water to wash it off and finds blood on her hands.

This time when she retches everything comes up.

She slouches out of the bathroom and sees what she hadn't the first time through the apartment. Pages. The first couple written in ink relatively new in appearance, the rest on stock so old and gray it looks like the peeled-away layers of a wasps' nest. Sheets roughly torn from a journal, a stack of them on her tiny dining room table against the wall outside the kitchen, the only thing on its surface other than her ceramic rooster-and-chicken salt and pepper shakers.

The handwriting is his. She's sure of it. The formal cursive, faded by time, the exposure to sun and redryings from the occasions rain found the paper, leaving craters of blurred ink behind.

Before she decides whether she should or not, she reads the first page.

And stops.

She searches every room of the apartment again, as if his words in her head are capable of materializing him out of thin air. In the kitchen, she wipes the counter with a sponge until it can hold no more before squeezing the blood out into the sink. She drops it as if only now recognizing its scalding heat, pours dish detergent over it, and turns on the tap. The water pinkening and swirling down the drain.

She goes to her bedroom and opens the jewelry box where her pills are. Over the months—has it been longer?—she's talked herself into seeing her relationship to them as essentially harmless, no more worrying than an after-work glass of wine or secret cigarette on a tough day. She takes them so occasionally and in such low doses they work as a placebo more than anything else. Still, she never opens the box that keeps her few sets of earrings and necklaces and pulls out the prescription bottle without a thrill of shame.

Every time Lily holds a tablet in her palm she thinks of her mother. This was her drug too.

It's all in the coroner's report. Her history of turnstiling in and out of psych wards across the country for vaguely described "episodes," the refusal of extended treatment, the resistance to any naming of her condition. And Haloperidol. The antipsychotic she stuck with the longest, though only God knows whether it helped or not.

Lily opens the bottle, shakes out a white tab. Swallows it dry.

He was here.

She looks around her bedroom as if it was lit by a blinding new light.

The psycho was in your apartment. You get that?

She feels the drug dissolving, spreading out through her blood. Silencing. Soon her head will be muffled. But not before one last declaration of fact.

He. Was. Here.

Who is he?

A man who sees himself in supernatural terms. She has had clients who've believed themselves superheroes, demons, time travelers. This one's claims are relatively conservative by comparison.

It would be easy to diagnose him—humanize him completely in her mind—if not for the fact that Lily has seen a real monster once.

And now, in a bolt of memory, she sees it again. The hulking, bent shape of it in the cabin's open doorway. The billows of hot breath exploding from its nostrils. The eyes yellow and sticky as if weeping an infectious discharge.

The man who killed Dr. Edmundston wasn't the monster. The creature the six-year-old Lily Dominick saw standing over her mother was bigger, stronger, inhuman. Yet hadn't the man clenched Dr. Edmundston's shoulder with a steel claw? Hadn't he placed a set of needle-sharp dentures into his mouth before tearing into the skin of her mentor's throat?

It's true that the man who murdered Lionel Edmundston has a most extraordinary mental disorder, one who takes his delusion of monstrosity so seriously he has fashioned tools to transform himself, a killing costume. But anyone with a glove of blades and syringes for incisors and a sufficiently diseased mind could have pulled off the same trick. You don't have to be immortal to be sick.

Otherwise, his connection to her is coincidental. Some research on her parents' names. An escape. He must have gone to a place where he knew Edmundston would be, a bar where men meet other men perhaps, and the two went back to his apartment together. Which is where Lionel's nightmare began.

He hadn't hypnotized her. He'd stepped toward her, a woman who had just witnessed a horrific attack, and she blacked out. Then he daubed incriminating blood on her, took their phones, and proceeded to her apartment where he found a way in and addressed his insane confession to her.

A confession she could show to the police. But who would believe it? She was there, saw all of it happen, and she can barely believe it herself.

And he has her knife.

Which means what, Doctor? Which means you do what?

Lily drifts over to the apartment's living room window that looks down onto 111th Street. Either he's an expert locksmith or he came in this way. There's a fire escape screwed into the brick fifteen feet to the left and a narrow ledge running the length of the exterior wall. It's possible he climbed up by that route and shimmied along to her window, pulling it open. All you'd need is good balance and the absence of fear.

Here.

This is what brings the vertigo, sends her back to sit at the table, her hands clenching the sides as if she is reaching the top of a roller coaster and beginning the descent. *He was here.* The man she'd recognized as different from the rest got out of the Kirby and came to sit in the chair she sits in now. Which makes everything he's done all about her.

She looks at her landline phone on the sofa, resting there like a cat in a pale band of dawn sunlight. The police would take her out of this. They would know what to do next.

But she doesn't move. Not yet.

Soon, the phone will ring. Someone from the Kirby will tell her one of her clients broke out. She will be advised to be cautious—a warning the hospital is required to give employees in situations of this kind. Later, someone will find Dr. Edmundston's body. In the morgue they will discover the strange puncture wounds in the neck along with the larger wounds to the body. But before that, minutes from now, when the sun is high enough it can't hide behind the building across the street anymore and her apartment brightens, she will tell the police everything she saw, everything she knows.

Or she won't.

There's still time to decide.

Still time to read the pages he left for her.

New York
June 16, 2016

I am not a myth. Not a story, fairy tale, or legend.

I am not a human being, though I am almost always mistaken for one, and am composed of human parts, among other things, some I understand and others that remain uncanny, even to me.

A name.

Sometimes I wonder if it's better that I don't have one. There's a power in that which is only occasionally glimpsed, tiny pieces of witnessed reality that force one into imagining the whole. Over the centuries it has been different things: gods, dragons, witches. It's one of the reasons I have elected to carry on.

For now, the world can call me by my preferred alias. The warrior angel.

Michael.

There are books about me. Classics of their kind. I am Michael in none of them, but it is me who stands behind their fabrications nonetheless. It is my life's work, though I have gone unacknowledged for my part in it.

Victor F.'s unnamed creature. Dr. Jekyll's other self. The Transylvanian Count.

Shelley, Stevenson, Stoker.

They have their fame, though it cannot reach them where they are now, down in the cold dirt of their graves. Unlike them, I am alive.

And unlike the monsters they are credited with creating, I am real.

London
October 12, 1812

How to begin, when one was made and not born?

Everything is in question, I see now, when it comes to telling a story. What to include and omit, where to linger, the moments to pronounce as turning points. Who to deem the hero and the villain.

Not least, in what language ought this strange document be written? Though it will remain forever private, I nevertheless see this record as belonging to the world, so I am inclined to dictate in the speech of the land where I now find myself. The first books I read were what the doctor happened to bring me from the floors of the house above my prison: anatomical texts, the poems of Berzsenyi, the Bible. But also a selection of Shakespeare's plays in English. He couldn't read it, and must have viewed his giving it to me as an empty gesture, or perhaps a joke at my expense. But I learned the language of the Bard through repeated study, and since modified it to match the talk of the high street, pub, and bawdy house over these past weeks wandering the lengths of England.

So, to begin. Begin at the beginning.

I was made in the cellar of the Chief Physician's residence on the grounds of the Lipótmezei Sanatorium on the outskirts of Budapest sometime in the fall of 1811.

Every other human being understands their Creator to be an all-powerful abstraction, caring and in possession of a plan for your existence. I, on the other hand, was created by a man, one with a dark beard and whose breath smelled of onions.

What I know of my making is limited to what the doctor—Dr. Tivadar Eszes— told me, which, while I have no reason to believe untrue, is certainly incomplete.

Given the authority he had over the operation in the hills off Huvösvölgyi Road, he had unquestioned access to every building, every ward, every room. Every patient.

For some years Dr. Eszes had been conducting experiments in the basement of his residence, a handsome yellow structure in the baroque style directly overlooking the main hospital. To be a doctor in that country—and especially the head of the national madhouse—was to conduct ad hoc trials of all types. Some of the procedures I witnessed would not be out of place in the torture rooms of the medieval past. Brain surgeries conducted by way of sinus or ear canal. Mercury and lead given as medicine. To say nothing of the more casual degradations of the asylum: starvation, castration, rape.

But Dr. Eszes was a man of unique inventiveness. His prescriptions went a good deal further than the ingestion of this oil over that beetle, or recommending hysterectomy here over a bloodletting there. He was ambitious in the truest sense, which is to say he may have been insane himself.

Outside of his official responsibilities of housing and treating the most damaged minds of Hungary, his prevailing obsession was to return life to the dead. And more than this: to invest this reanimated creature with features of superhuman enhancement. Greater strength, intelligence. Hypnotic powers of persuasion. The most acute animal reflexes and instincts. Immortality too. His thinking was that if he could assemble such a being, a working prototype he could parade before the leadership in government, he would be given the resources to make an army of them. Refined Magyar blood emanating from the Hungarian capital and spreading over the map of Europe! Dr. Eszes was nothing if not a patriot. A sadist too. A genius. For isn't genius defined by the capacity to create something without precedent?

The good doctor would use his patients for raw material. This gave him the advantage of access, as each new corpse could be delivered to his home within minutes of their final breaths. The disadvantage was that drawing bodies from this pool meant he was working from faulty parts from the outset.

Yet even in this he was confident he had a solution. He required only the body to be human. The skin, bones, face. To this he would add the blood of what he considered to be the perfect animal, along with a serum of his own devising injected via the orbit of the eye. The result was intended to be much more than the parlor trick of bringing a dead lunatic back to life. It was an altogether new and better creature he foresaw rising from the gore-slick slab! It was Hungary itself—ever divided, ever claimed and abandoned by outsiders—united in a man-that-is-better-than-man!

I was, one year ago, that creature who rose from the slab.

Needless to say, the result was not exactly as the doctor had envisioned.

Of all the things that could have prevented his success it wasn't the biological or chemical or surgical processes that failed him. It was a disease of the spirit.

Just as science's greatest achievement stood before him, Dr. Eszes looked into my eyes and instantly saw a wrongness. Not the soul of a superman, but the dead stare of a devil.

My creator was an alienist. An expert on diseases of the mind. He was also an alchemist, perhaps the last of them, and in creating me, the greatest of them.

Dr. Eszes stood on the line that marked the end of primitive sorcery and the beginning of modern science. We are alike in this, the doctor and me. "Father" and "son." For as much as I am a creature of chemistry, I am also the embodiment of the demonic, a presence that is older than Earth itself.

The one patient of Dr. Eszes's who was used in my assembly—the donor body—was a young murderer who was said to have been possessed. Even after a rite of exorcism was performed on Peter Farkas by the priest in the town of Csány where he'd been born to a good family, the demon mocked the priest and the witnesses assembled. The spirit told them it would never release the child no matter what prayers they might chant, because it had a plan for him, one whose fruits they would all come to see for themselves. And I believe it can be said that they did.

Peter Farkas had never gone to school. His parents provided the boy with sustenance but kept him mostly in his room. The townsfolk were co-conspirators in his neglect. When he howled and cursed through his open window, they walked past without looking, as if they heard only birdsong.

Eventually, the boy grew into a man. Reasoning that he was no longer their responsibility, Farkas's father transported him to the farming village of Szarvas on the southern plains and left him there to find employment. And, indeed, Peter soon discovered his true vocation.

Moving from place to place, sleeping in thickets and in paddock corners, killing and feeding on the fruits of the hunt. An acceptable way to survive if what he hunted wasn't human.

Dr. Eszes owned a country house outside Budapest in the Bükk Hills, in the village of Szilvásvárad. There he kept

9

It stops there.

Lily goes to the window and pulls it open, sticks her head out, and scans the block in both directions. She half expects him to still be down there, waiting on the corner so he can wave up at her before slipping away.

Psycho.

A two-hundred-year-old man who believes he personally inspired *Frankenstein, Strange Case of Dr. Jekyll and Mr. Hyde, Dracula.*

If not human, what are you?

A psychopath like all the others. More imaginative than most, but this remains the only answer. What prevents Lily from wholly believing it is how he knows her secret. The one so veiled it remained hidden even from herself.

I am not a myth.

Lily starts to shake and can't stop. *This is shock,* she tells herself. The last twenty-four hours fracturing into voices, phrases written on ancient paper. A horrific collage.

I am a singular case.

The man stepping out of Lionel's kitchen.

I'm here to give you a gift.

The silver teeth.

If it's a secret, it's been sitting right under mankind's nose for a very long time.

Lily looks down at the handwritten note—the one drafted in her apartment, warning her not to call the police—and notices for the first time something written on the back.

Budapest

The phone rings behind her.

She looks out at her corner of the city, the new sun yellowing the brick and concrete, and cars beetling in the buttery light. The faint smell of roasted chestnuts and sewage she thinks of as New York's unique cologne. Along with something else she tells herself she's only imagining. Something animal. The wet straw and horses' breath of a stable.

PART 2

The Old World

10

Lily keeps expecting to spot him among the mourners at Dr. Edmundston's funeral. She knows it would be an incredible risk for him to show up given the ongoing police manhunt for him, just five days after the murder. On the other hand, he's insane.

The fact is, Lily has been looking for him since the morning she'd finished reading the pages from his journal. Starting from her walk to the Kirby to endure several hours of going about her work, pretending she didn't know Dr. Edmundston had been killed until, at day's end, Denise burst into her office in tears to repeat the e-mail that had been distributed among the staff. Found dead in his apartment. Evidence of foul play. Police investigating. Coworkers with any information urged to come forward.

"Sounds like something bad happened," Denise said. "Like *bad* bad."

"Oh my God."

"That sweet man."

"It's awful."

"You okay? You look like—"

"I think I have to go home."

"Sure."

"Can you cover my appointments? I just—"

"Absolutely."

She gave Denise a hug on the way out. That's when Lily wept—not in horror, but grief alone.

"I'll call you," Lily said, willing herself to pull away and walk out into the hall.

It was the last time she would ever see Denise or her office again.

She looked for him on the walk home. Then from her window through the rest of the afternoon. And later too, on her night run to the store to buy juice, bread, and Kleenex. Even as she lay down on her bed, not expecting sleep but wanting to be ready for it if she got lucky, she opened her eyes from time to time to see if the man who called himself Michael emerged from the shadows of her room.

Find him, her voice urged.

He has the knife. So long as he held on to it, she was his.

Then get it back.

"How?" she says aloud. "I'd be better off calling a lawyer."

A lawyer won't help if the knife ends up with the police. And a lawyer can't tell you what Michael says he can about who you are. Who your mother was.

"He doesn't know me."

The only way you'll be sure of that is to go to him.

"Why should I do what he wants?"
Because it's what you want too.

When a detective left his number she called back straight away.

It was harder than she would have guessed to separate what she actually knew from what was safe to tell him. It should have been easy to pronounce a lie as simple as "I don't know anything." But once she deviated from the truth and told the detective how she left her date's apartment in the middle of the night and had gone home to sleep in her own bed ("You do that a lot?" he asked, and she'd answered, "I like my bed.") the words sounded awkward as a foreign language she'd only begun to learn.

Two days after Edmundston's funeral, she called the Kirby's personnel director and asked for a leave of absence. Lily imagined the pitying look on the woman's face. It was the look she always wore. Lily figured it came with all the firing she had to do.

"As you know, Doctor," the woman started, "bereavement leave is available only in case of loss of immediate family."

"I'm not expecting to be paid," Lily said.

"I see."

"And I don't know when I'll be back."

A long sigh blew down the line and into Lily's

ear. "That puts us in something of a situation, doesn't it? Dr. Edmundston is of course gone, and now you—I mean, the *department*—"

"I just need some time."

"Is this about what happened? To Dr. Edmundston? Should we be making a claim—insurance, there's a process. Are you suffering from feelings of fear? Anxiety?"

"Do I have to tell you if I am?"

"I suppose not. No."

"Then let's just call this an indefinite unpaid leave."

Lily hung up before she could say something regrettable.

She rereads Michael's journal pages so many times she finds herself switching between two points of view. As a psychiatrist, she sees it as the articulation of a highly developed personality disorder, one that has devised an identity with its own impossible origin story. But then she reads it again and sees how at least some of it might be true.

I am not a human being, though I am almost always mistaken for one.

Lily doesn't think for a second that Michael came to life in 1811. But perhaps he is Hungarian. And perhaps his psychosis was thought to be demonic possession by his family in his youth (it wouldn't be the first time she's dealt with a client and their spouses or parents who believe their condition has a supernatural basis).

Perhaps, after coming to America, Michael somehow met Lily's mother.

Maybe they came across each other in a hospital or halfway house somewhere. Given his age, he would probably have been the child of a fellow patient, but old enough to talk to her, remember her. She herself knows little about her mother other than, after Lily was born, the two of them moved from trailer park to motel room to the cabin up north. It was a nomadic existence that came from being poor. But there was more to it than just that. The medications, for one thing. Off and on, on and off. Most likely a paranoid, like Michael. In her case, it was the belief that there were people after her. Lily has the vaguest memory of asking what people they were.

"The ones who *know,*" her mother said.

For Lily, her mother's mental illness has a taste: the bitter tea and, even worse, the soups she was made to eat as a child. They were concoctions her mother must have made from things she collected from the forest floor, because Lily has no memory of them ever visiting a health food store, and the cabin in Alaska was nowhere near such a place anyway. The taste of the food, recalled decades later, sickens Lily, but it also makes her angry, as if her mother's broths were meant to do more than nourish her. Were they a New Age, anti-vaxer medicine of some kind? Were they a punishment?

Lily reads the pages all over again.

Made, not born.

Michael isn't two hundred and five years old. He's not the inspiration for the three most regarded gothic novels of the nineteenth century. He was not created by an alienist, but came into the world the same as everyone else. He's not her father.

But it's possible that he knows something about her mother that she doesn't know herself.

Denise is the only person Lily calls to say she's going away for a while. She felt someone ought to know. But as soon as she's telling her that the loss of Dr. Edmundston has hit her hard and that she's decided to take some time off, it all feels wrong.

"Where will you go?" Denise asks, her voice camouflaging her alarm.

"I don't know yet. I figured I'd just head to the airport and pick somewhere off the departures board."

"That doesn't sound like you."

"I think that's why I want to do it."

"Is this about Lionel?" Denise asks. "Or is there something else going on?"

"What do you mean, something else?"

"You just—you sound scared. And it's not like you to be scared."

"My friend just died. Was murdered. Probably by someone I met with. Don't you think I should be scared?"

"You think I ought to be too?"

"He won't come back to the Kirby," Lily says, and as soon as she does, believes it to be true.

"Why not?"

"I do profiles for a living."

"So what? That make you a mind reader?"

Depends on the mind, she thinks but doesn't say.

"I'll see you when I get back," Lily says.

"You be careful."

"Always."

She's zipping up her suitcase when she gets the crank call.

That's how Lily tries to think of it afterward, working to convince herself that there's no connection between the events of the past several days that have pulled her clear of her normal life and the stranger on the phone, asking if she is Dr. Lily Dominick without offering his own name.

"Who is this?"

"We need to meet."

"Did that dating site give you my number? If they—"

"I want to protect you."

"—this is illegal solicitation. I was told my privacy would—"

"You're not safe."

The man's voice is deep, exuding professional authority. Lily imagines the man such a voice would belong to and sees him as physically commanding, handsome. It's almost enough to distract her from the frightening thing he's just said.

"That's a threat," she says. "Also illegal."

"Listen to me. There isn't much time. What's going on—it's not anything like what you think it is. But I can't—others could already be listening. Just name a location and go straight there. I'll meet you. What I—"

"Who *is* this?"

"My name is Will," the voice says. "We have something in common. Someone. Just give me a—"

She hangs up. After she sees that the incoming caller's number was blocked, she pulls the phone's cord from the wall before he can call again.

A scam artist. Her personal info hacked from a website account. A prankster making a couple broad guesses that would hit a target with virtually anyone. *We have something in common. Someone.* Lily dismisses the caller as any one of these but doesn't quite believe it.

She can feel him trying to call her back and

considers plugging the phone back in if only to hear his at once urgent and comforting voice again, but in the end she leaves to avoid giving it any more thought and goes downstairs to hail a cab to the airport.

At JFK she finds a bookstore and heads straight to the Classics section. Picks out *Frankenstein, Strange Case of Dr. Jekyll and Mr. Hyde,* and *Dracula.*

"Guess you don't plan on sleeping through your flight," the cashier says.

At her gate Lily waits to board and opens *Frankenstein.*

> You will rejoice to hear that no disaster has accompanied the commencement of an enterprise which you have regarded with such evil forebodings. . . .

No disaster yet, maybe, her inner voice says. *But no shortage of evil forebodings.*

A moment later they're calling her flight to Frankfurt. She's never been there. She's never been anywhere in Europe before. But Frankfurt isn't her final destination. It's there that she'll get her connecting flight to Budapest.

11

She finishes the first book halfway over the Atlantic. In Frankfurt her connecting flight is delayed four hours, which gives her time to read the other two. Given the jet lag and subject matter, she arrives in Budapest frightened and wired.

There's the feeling that she's not only traveling east but back in time. Her first glimpses of Eastern Europe support this impression: the bare trees plumped with the pom-poms of squirrels' nests, the Soviet-era factories and fields of clumped soil. All of it viewed through a haze of rain, the dawn fogged and colorless.

The spell is only half-broken when she checks in to her hotel on the Pest side of the river. Once in her room she showers, takes one of her pills, and slips under the comforter with a wish for dreamless sleep, though she dreams nonetheless.

"Put the butt against your shoulder. Hard, like that."

Her mother's voice is so clear Lily is sure she's dead. They're both dead. Which makes this her first step into eternity.

She is six years old again and being taught how to hold a gun.

"Press it to your cheek so you can see straight down to the end. Close that eye and keep that one open. See?"

Lily feels the cool wood of the stock against her face. The rifle is heavy but it's a weight she can manage, the length of it steady in her hands. She aims it into the darkness. Is it night? Are they outside? She can hear her mother, feel her close, but she's just behind her and to the side so she can't see her.

"Mama?"

"Yes, muffin?"

"How do I shoot?"

"Your finger through there. Feel that? But you only pull if you're sure that everything's right."

"Why?"

"Because you can't take it back."

She can't see anything but finds a target in the dark all the same. The rifle goes still. Something inside her holds the aim, absorbs all her fear.

"You're ready," her mother says.

The next morning, after room service fried eggs, she walks out to a taxi stand and gives the driver an address. He replies in Hungarian, which sounds to Lily like a combination of Chinese, Portuguese, and Russian. She can't help hearing odd English words and phrases randomly repeated in it. *Catfish,* for one. Along with *sequence* and *told you* and, more than anything else, *hashtag*.

"Hospital," she clarifies. "The old asylum. Where they put the crazy people?"

He looks at her as if she herself is crazy before shrugging and driving off.

Michael told her to come to Budapest and now that she's here, she's going to the only place he mentioned in the pages he left for her. Where it started. In his mind, anyway. To get the knife back she has to think like he does.

And to ask him about your mother you have to find him.

The taxi crosses the Chain Bridge over the Danube and heads north up the long slope of the Huvösvölgyi Road. After a mile or two the city yields to larger properties that Lily guesses may be private schools or embassies. It's uphill the whole way and yet, when she looks back through the rear window, the elevation affords her no view.

The driver pulls into a small parking lot and stops. All Lily can see that would suggest arrival at her destination is a bus shelter by the road and a stucco gatehouse with a chain blocking any vehicle's way up a lane that's soon consumed by untamed shrubs.

"Catfish hashtag," the driver seems to say.

Lily checks the fare on the meter, the numbers in forints making no sense to her. She offers him fifty euros and he shakes his head at her excess, but offers no change.

Once she's out of the car and the driver has started back down the road Lily finds herself alone. While the occasional car still roars past there is no one on the sidewalk or in the bus shelter. There are curtains in the gatehouse's grimy window and an empty can of beer by the door, but nobody comes out.

"Hello?" she says, this single word of English sounding foolish in the gray air.

She decides to keep going until somebody stops her. And if that happens, she'll play dumb. Pretend she's a tourist with a thing for old madhouses. She hopes there's enough euros in her pocket to work as a bribe if she's charged with trespassing.

She steps over the chain and starts up the cracked entry lane. A funny security system, if that's what this is, because she sees now a high fence heading off in both directions around the grounds, its top garlanded with razor wire.

Soon the lane splits in two and Lily goes up a walkway through what was likely once a garden. She keeps waiting to hear a voice demanding to know where she thinks she's going, but proceeds up the first set of steps without interruption before being swallowed by the tunnel of interlocked branches an arm's length over her head.

The thought that nobody knows she's here

crosses her mind. Someone could attack or imprison or kill her without a living soul on this side of the Atlantic wondering what happened to her, her existence erased so easily because she's half erased it herself. This worry almost turns her around. But then the main hospital building appears and she decides, having come this far, to take a closer look.

It would have been stately in the past. A distinguished, imposing architecture for what, a couple centuries ago, was designed to accommodate all of Hungary's most severely mentally ill. Lily guesses that from the gate you could barely hear the howls and cries even when the windows were opened in the summer.

She tries the front doors. They give a half-inch but no more, chained shut from the inside.

By the looks of it, this place hasn't been a functioning hospital for decades. According to Michael's story, one of the long-ago inmates was Peter Farkas. But Farkas only became Michael in Dr. Eszes's residence, not here.

She carries on to the right and along the front of the main building and spots the house facing the hospital from a level rise. Made of the same yellow stone, but with an arched colonnade along the front that gives it the look of a stern mouth.

Lily climbs up the hill, its deceptive steepness forcing her hands as well as her feet to grab and push at the soft earth. At the top she has to fight the temptation to lie down. Whether it's nerves or a change in altitude, breathing requires a conscious effort.

She wants to go.

You want to know.

The cellar.

That's why she's here. It's not enough to be on the ground where Michael's fiction is set. She has to go inside.

Unlike the main building, the front doors of the doctor's residence are chained from the outside. The windows along the colonnade are mostly smashed, with bars on the interior. Lily makes her way around the side, looking for a way in.

At the rear, there's a single door, three brick steps leading into the ground. The door almost certainly locked too, but she knows her inner voice will call her chicken shit if she doesn't at least try it.

It gives at the touch of her hand.

The air reeks of mildew and cat urine and something chemical like formaldehyde. It makes her cough as she enters. The sound of it is still reverberating off the walls when it's followed by a shuffling she tells herself is only the retreat of a rat or some other vermin.

She stands at one end of a hallway with door-ways opening onto different rooms on either side. The floor is littered with empty cigarette packs, dead leaves, food wrappers. An inch from the toe of her foot is a used syringe.

Lily remembers the flashlight function on the pay-as-you-go cell phone she bought when she landed, pulls it out of her back pocket, and turns it on.

For a second, it captures movement at the end of the hall.

The shuffling again. This time clearer, like someone balling up newspaper in their hands. But when she holds the phone steady there's just the confirmation of her first impression: a hall with rooms she can't see inside unless she takes a step into them.

What now, psycho?

Her foot is rising over the syringe and planting its first step on the floor before she realizes she's made any decision to go forward. The smell grows stronger. It makes her think of traveling down into the stomach of a sleeping beast, the reek of its breath blowing into her face.

She shines the cell phone's light into the first room and finds a random collection of rusted chairs in a semicircle, as if a group therapy session abruptly ended fifty years ago. The next room houses the boiler. Vents growing out of it and reaching through the ceiling into the floors above.

The third room is the largest. Lily can feel the size of it before she looks inside, the cold distance between herself and the walls expanding into starless space. This is where the odor is coming from. It occurs to her now that the smell is that of a morgue.

She steps into the widening darkness. Her legs sinking, pulling her down through the house's foundation into the soil below.

The cell phone's light is cast at her feet. Lily moves the beam across the far brick wall.

Legs. Blue eyes. Dark curly hair. Naked skin.

Lily extends her arms and locks her elbows in place. Forces the light to shine on the thing in the corner.

An infant doll. Propped so that its legs are stretched in front of it, its eyes bright marbles of surprise. A girl.

Run.

But something prevents her. The doll's arms are wrapped around an envelope. She steps closer and squints at the partly obscured writing on the outside. An L at the beginning and Y at the end. Her name.

The doll is meant for her. The doll *is* her.

She swings the cell phone's light around. Broken furniture assembled in a mound as if in readiness to be ignited in a pyre. A winking spray of broken glass on the floor. A wheelchair with green water pooled in its seat.

The circle of light narrows and at first Lily thinks her vision is failing, that she's blacking out as she did in Dr. Edmundston's apartment. But soon the light casts only a sepia circle on the floor directly in front of her. The battery. Already drained of whatever power came with it upon purchase.

She moves toward the doll, picks it up. Then the light on her phone goes out.

Lily freezes, listening. Much closer than before, the shuffling again.

She turns the cell phone off and on. As it reboots, the light returns in a momentary flash. One that reveals a man in the opposite corner of the room. His silver teeth a line of ice in his mouth.

The light dies.

She slams into the far wall, scrambling away. Her hands frantically slap at the wood of a door.

"Please, God. *Please . . .*"

She finds the handle and pulls it open, scrambles up the steps and trips on the raised edge of brick at the top, rolling a few feet over the gravel.

Her eyes stay on the darkness beyond the open cellar door. She lies there, the air whistling in and out of her lungs, waiting for something to emerge. Yet when she senses movement it's not from the cellar, but the far corner of the building.

The dog stops at the same time Lily sets her eyes on it. A German shepherd mixed with something else, one of the breeds with oversized heads, the jaws meant to clamp shut and never open. It doesn't growl. Just shows its teeth like the man in the cellar had done, its pink jowls trembling.

Stay still.

"Get up."

Her body obeys her spoken voice. She doesn't take her eyes from the motionless dog. On her second step, it lowers its ears against its head.

On her third step, it comes at her.

Lily runs. Not through the tunnel of branches this time but straight for the road.

The dog catches up to her before she makes it to the laneway down to the road. With every stride it jumps forward so that it comes up alongside her and she see its tartar-coated teeth, the eyes jellied with rage.

She drops the doll but not the envelope. It's not intentional, it just slips free from her hand. But once it's falling, Lily hopes it will distract the dog. Maybe it will stop to tear its limbs off and not hers. Instead the doll bounces harmlessly off the animal's back.

The gatehouse is a hundred yards away. Across the road a mother pushes a stroller along the opposite sidewalk, watching Lily with an expression that could be either alarm or amusement.

You're safe, lady, Lily thinks. *I should be over there with you.*

Just when Lily begins to entertain the hope that the dog is trained only to bark and not bite, its teeth find the back of her leg.

Her arms spinning like rotor blades. The dog spins with her. Round to the front and then kicked behind again, the motion so intricately balanced between the two of them it might appear to be rehearsed, an interspecies dance.

With one heaving turn she throws the dog off. Lily takes a breath. The pain screams from her ankle and up her throat.

The noise triggers the dog to come at her again. This time, instead of running, she kicks at it with her good foot. The toe of her shoe clips its jaw.

The impact knocks the animal back onto its haunches, its mouth opening and closing as if checking to see if anything's broken. It gives Lily a chance to go for the gatehouse.

She hurdles over the chain across the entrance, her bad foot coming down first, the ankle buckling, sending her to the pavement. The dog could have her now. Lily readies herself for it, holding the crinkled envelope uselessly against her face.

Nothing happens.

When Lily looks, the dog remains on the other side of the chain, panting.

"You're not allowed off your property, that it?" Lily says to the animal as she gets to her feet again. "It's all yours."

She makes her way to the sidewalk, the mother with the stroller now openly staring at her. The voice inside her wants to shout across the road and tell the woman where she can stick it, but Lily resists and limps on, not even looking for a cab to hail, and starts down the hill into the city.

Cornwall, England
November 22, 1812

"You are my secret."

These were the first words I remember Eszes saying to me, as if announcing me as such bound me to remain so.

For a long time I saw no one but the doctor. I was kept to the laboratory, slept on a pallet he'd left on the floor, stared with disgust at the food he would place at the small table I was meant to dine at.

Even if I had been capable of love I wouldn't have loved the doctor. I considered him a jailer more than a companion. My repeated request was to leave the house and see what lay beyond its walls. For many days the doctor would reply that such freedoms would follow after a period of observation. When I protested that it was beyond his power to treat me as a farmer would his livestock, he corrected me.

"You are my creation," he said. "If you were to leave this place without my consent, I would be forced to destroy you, because it cannot be known you exist. In time, we will be celebrated. But for now, we are criminals. Original sinners."

I tried to see this commonality as friendship, but felt only that the doctor's analogy failed to apply to me. He committed a blasphemy by giving me life, but I was merely alive, faultless. In any case, how would the laws of man apply to a being who was not a man?

The doctor never spoke of me by name. He never gave me one.

Whether in his absence or presence, I soon wished to kill him. In part because this was an aspect of my emerging nature, in part because I was tired of the bottles of horse blood he brought me for nourishment. Like an eaglet, I was no longer content to open my mouth and have my parent fill it, but longed to feed myself.

The smell of the doctor's skin brought it on, the pumping of his heart audible to me before he opened the door. I would look at him and think of the ways I would open him up to expose the warm life within. It would have happened there, in that lightless cellar, if there weren't things I needed to learn from him.

It was quickly discovered that the experiment had yielded at least one unexpected result. Although I inhabited the body of a dead man, in his resuscitation his old mind had been left behind and the new one open to be its own thing. Mine. This seemed to be a mystery even to the doctor. He anticipated that his process would produce a brain of greater capacity but would remain in character more or less the same as Peter Farkas's, the one whose neck the doctor had wrapped a chain around and choked the life out of. For this is what Eszes decided was necessary. Not to wait until a patient died of natural causes, as he had been doing up until then, but the freshness of new death, of murder.

Yet there was little of Farkas left in me. A handful of memories. Some excited recollection of the faces of those he murdered in their final moments. Playing hide-and-seek with his younger sister when they were children. His mother's voice. It was, to me, distant in the way of a story one has been told long ago and forgotten the ending to.

The alienist in the doctor was fascinated

by this. I could see it in his eyes when he looked upon me. Who was this man who sat at the table with him, his manners refined, his hunger not for the food laid before him but for knowledge, for books? I cannot explain it myself, though I have my theories. A personality is a different thing from a mind. It is experience. You take that away and you become something with the capacity for thought but without the programming imposed by parents, school, social interaction. I am a man liberated from the rules of humanity.

I was a child with the faculties of an adult, free to create my own inclinations. But there were other ingredients within me now too. Animal blood. Specifically, the blood of horses. The Lipizzaner breed that the doctor kept in his stables in Szilvásvárad. Their hides a brilliant white, their proud stock going back to the warrior Huns. The Lipizzans' blood lent me strength and endurance and speed, attributes the doctor so admired.

And it worked, up to a point. But the combination of these chemicals and memories and the spiritual parasite that clung to my soul and a hunger for blood to sustain me resulted in a whole new man, and not merely an improved version of Peter Farkas.

"Do you look at me and see me as a child might see his father?" the doctor once asked, and as I record the words of his query on this page it returns our conversation so clearly it is as if it occurred this morning.

"No."

"Tell me then." He held a mirror before my face. "What do you see?"

"A mask."

"But it is your face. You mean a mask in the metaphorical sense."

"I suppose, yes."

"What would be revealed if I were to remove it?"

"That I couldn't say."

"Why not?"

"Because I don't know myself yet. Whatever it is, it grows closer to what I wish to become."

"And what is it you wish to become?"

"There is no name for it. I suppose the closest thing would be a god."

"A god of benevolence, or a god of war?"

"Those are human terms on a human spectrum. They don't define me."

The doctor laughed at that. An unpleasant,

mocking laugh. "Perhaps you require your own language!"

"I believe you're right, Doctor. To understand me is to speak a new language. One I will have to invent."

"Oh, very fine," the old sadist said. "But who would you speak it with? Who would comprehend your meaning?"

"There will soon be others like me. This is your intention, is it not?"

"That will depend upon your success."

"Success?"

"At keeping your mask on."

He was wrong in so many ways, and though I hated him for it, in this Dr. Eszes would prove correct.

He promised I would not be alone.

It was not merely a bride I longed for, but the society of others like myself. A family. The only way to know myself was through the reflections in my fellow creatures' eyes, a vision no looking glass could provide. To be a "mate," a "friend," a "father": What would such performances require to be convincing?

I yearned to be tested on the field of passions. It was unclear if I had the capacity to duplicate what the poets celebrated. Could I self-sacrifice, woo, inspire? Could I see another's life as something more than an invitation to destruction? Could I love?

Instead of keeping his word, the doctor's visits grew less frequent. His attitude toward me changed from thrilled triumph, to scientific scrutiny, to an unshakeable gloom.

"Put this on," he said finally. From his coat pocket he produced a wool hood. "Nobody can see your face until we arrive at our destination."

The hood felt thick, and it would be airless and hot inside. Was I being taken to freedom, or to my execution?

I put it on. Even through the black wool I could smell his skin, his blood.

I asked where he was taking me as he nudged me up the stairs. He answered that we were to journey into the country, and when I suggested it was there he planned on releasing me he said nothing. He didn't have to.

It was as if his mind were speaking directly to my own. He would never let me go. I had been brought back from the dead, but now that I was alive, he was confronting the meaning of his accomplishment. He would never present me to his superiors, never propose an army of the undead to the Hungarian parliament. It was absurd to even think it.

A dragon may be wondrous to behold, but that same wonder demands it be slain.

When Dr. Eszes removed the hood several hours later in the carriage we rode in, the world exploded in color. Green, mostly. Forests that rolled out on either side of us. The road followed a creek, its gray water turned white as it passed over the rocks that poked through like partly buried skulls.

I asked the doctor again where he was taking me.

"To my country house. You will be presented as a hired servant. To work with the groomsman."

"Is this where your family resides? Will I meet them?"

If the doctor had appeared uneasy before, his complexion now whitened to match the hair of the horses he so treasured.

"You are married, Doctor? Children?"

He didn't want to answer. But he answered nevertheless.

"A wife. A twelve-year-old son."

"And you haven't told them how I came to be, have you?"

"No."

"Tell me, Doctor. What was the chemical you devised that brought me to life?"

He closed his eyes. Then he grabbed the hood and placed it once again over my head.

"That is something you will never learn," he said.

The poor man's voice came out in a boyish squeak that told us both where we now stood.

We arrived at the doctor's house in the night. He removed my hood, the world a chalky layering of shadows. Candles burned in the window of the main house, a beacon left for the doctor by his wife. But I was not to sleep there. Instead, he showed me to the servants' dwelling up the slope next to the stables.

My room was little more than a cell with a single mattress of straw, a water jug, and a bedpan.

I asked Eszes through the door if he really believed the chain he looped around the handle and key he turned in its lock would contain me.

"Goodnight," he said, ignoring my question.

"Goodnight, father."

I listened to him shuffle down the hall and start back to the house where his family slept, oblivious in their dreaming.

12

Lily makes it back to her hotel and reads the journal pages before she takes a better look at the bite on her leg. Not as bad as it feels. She judges the wound to be minor enough to get away without stitches, but it will need some antiseptic and bandages.

She gets directions to the nearest pharmacy from the concierge and makes her way across Erzsébet Square, where the pathway has been lined with temporary wood kiosks forming an early Christmas bazaar. Students, tourists, and locals jostle Lily in the tight space. Along with the folk art and handmade jewelry, there are stands selling cakes, sausage sandwiches, and mulled cider. The smells make her stomach flip.

She stops in the middle of the crowd, the events of the day forcing their way to the front of her mind. The doll in the corner of the cellar. The glimpse of silver teeth. A piece of a madman's memoir left for her on the other side of the world from where she was only two days ago, pages with *Look into the horses' eyes* handwritten on the back of their envelope.

A meaningless direction to anyone but Lily. It returns to her mind the memory of being carried from the cabin on the back of a white animal, one that left tracks that the Native American hunter she visited in Anchorage guessed to belong to a horse. Only a coincidence on the face of it, but Lily feels she can make it more than that if she just looks harder, goes further. A connection that's out there, waiting for her.

You don't know what the hell you're doing, do you? her inner voice asks before answering its own question. *You don't have a fucking clue. And it's going to get you killed.*

For the first time since leaving New York, the possibility that she's leading herself to her own end strikes her. Up until now, she's been in some form of self-delusion, a padded cell protecting her from the obvious. She's seen this before in her practice. Sometimes proximity to a horrific act lends a sense of immunity. It's why certain plane crash survivors take up skydiving, or war zone soldiers request additional tours of duty.

But even now she can't shake the idea that it's not Michael who will hurt her. He has a plan for her. And if his plan was merely to destroy her, he would have done that already.

There are many ways to die, her voice counters. *Some come fast, some come in time.*

115

She's here to find him. To follow the pull of her bones for once, her overlooked heart, to determine if he belongs to her by blood or not.

And what if he does kill her, what would it mean?

Tell me what the world would look like if you had never been born, Dr. Edmundston says, his voice coming to her from out of nowhere. Not his ghost, but one of his preferred lines of examination in client interviews she'd sat in on when she first arrived at the Kirby.

Then Edmundston asks the question directly of her.

Would anything be lost, Lily—anything at all— if you ceased to exist?

It makes her think of the baby.

She hadn't really thought of him for a good while now, but today Jonathan is with her. His pink face, the tiny hands grasping the air, reaching for her on the other side of the incubator's glass.

The pregnancy was something she went through alone for a few reasons. The first was that she had few close friends she could call on to go with her to prenatal classes or fetch the ketchup potato chips she had nocturnal cravings for. But what isolated her even more was embarrassment: a grad student having an affair with her married professor becomes pregnant and decides to have the baby. The most transformative moment of her life could only be preserved from cliché if no one found out who the father was.

"I can help," the professor had said when she told him. "With money, I mean. To handle things."

"Handle things?"

"I meant only—"

"I don't want any money."

He frowned. "Of course it's your *right,* but I wonder how public you intend to make all this?"

"It isn't a question I've considered."

"No. Well. Could you? Consider it, that is. From my point of view?"

He made it easy to walk away. It took this moment, however, for Lily to realize she'd never had much affection for the man, their entanglement built upon mutually satisfying manipulation more than attraction.

The fact was she didn't care about him. She was surprised to find that she wanted to have the baby as much as she'd been surprised to find herself pregnant in the first place. The whole thing made her happy in the most uncomplicated way. She presumed motherhood to be a series of obstacles one overcame in the name of duty or mindless biological imperative. For someone who saw emotions as thorny growths to be pruned, Lily's feelings toward the life inside her arrived instantly, inarguably.

On the day she learned she was carrying a boy

she named him Jonathan after the father she'd never met.

Even when her ob-gyn shared her concerns about the fetus's progress, Lily's usual pessimism was swept aside by breezy good spirits. If the baby was smaller than normal, well, so what? So was she.

Once Jonathan was born the news was worse.

A hole in his heart, the doctors told her. The valves so underdeveloped they couldn't pump the blood fast enough, the tiny muscle swamped. If he were older, stronger, there were long-shot procedures they might have tried, but as it was there was nothing they could do.

"Nothing they could do," Lily would find herself repeating over the years that followed her child's four days of life. She tried to wring some comfort out of it, prevent her grief from running away with itself by returning to the fact that his death was a foregone conclusion, with nobody to blame.

A hole in his heart now a hole in hers.

A trembling takes hold of Lily. She feels cold to the bone. Her fashionable leather jacket wasn't made to fend off the frigid drizzle of an Eastern European autumn. One of the bazaar's stands just ahead is selling bright red wool mittens and toques and she buys both. A hanging mirror reflects a queasy elf back at her.

It also reveals a man.

He is three stands behind her, studying sticks of maple candy in the offhand way of someone pretending interest. It's not Michael, it's not anyone she's seen before. A cleft chin, thin lips, wearing a black parka. It's not his looks but the absence of expression that fills her with fear. An aura of cruelty.

He glances her way, catches himself in the mirror—and Lily looking back at him—grabs three candy sticks, and fishes in his pocket to pay for them.

Lily rejoins the bazaar's stream of people, crosses the square, and runs against the light at the street on the far side. A delivery truck skids to a stop a few feet short of her, its driver rolling down the window to shout Hungarian curses. Down a narrow lane she spots the pointed spires of Szent István Bazilika. But when the lane opens onto the broad cobblestone square in front of the church, Lily sees she's made a mistake. If the man is following her, it will take her too long to cross the open space before he spots her.

There's a Starbucks on the corner and she slips inside, pushing her way through the crowd to the bathroom at the back. From here she can look through the windows at the basilica steps. The sound of American tourists ordering personalized lattes drowns the beating heart in her throat.

A moment later she sees the man.

Not running, but striding into the square. When

he doesn't see her he pauses, his eyes passing over the storefronts. He lingers on the Starbucks so long Lily wonders if he can see her flattened against the wall.

Now it's his body that communicates violence. Something in his sure gait, arms rigid at the shoulders.

He's not the police. He wants to destroy you.

He heads up the basilica steps to the right and through the open doors. She has to move. Now.

Lily keeps her head down as she leaves the café and starts back the way she came.

Don't turn around. If you do, you deserve whatever you get.

She turns around.

The black parka man steps out of the basilica and scans the square on all sides. Freezes when his eyes find her. His hand slips into the pocket of his parka and pulls out a gun.

Lily runs as fast as she can, her bitten leg sending electric shocks of pain with every pounding stride. She envisions the superior pace of Black Parka compared to her and glances back to confirm him starting down the same side street, eighty yards behind her, maybe less.

When she makes it to the street, she holds her arm high, hoping for a cab, for anybody to stop. A car without any sign on the roof pulls over. It could be one of the illegal taxis she read about in the guidebook. It could be someone working with the man in the black parka.

On impulse Lily gets in the backseat. Before she can look in the rearview mirror at whoever's driving, the car lurches forward.

Outside the window, Black Parka slows his run to a walk as he returns the gun to his pocket and watches her pull away. She's expecting him to shout some profanity, or raise his middle finger. But he does nothing.

"Where you go?" the driver asks in English.

"Just drive," Lily answers.

She pats her hands over her leather jacket and feels her passport, wallet, and phone inside— everything she needs. She won't return to the hotel. Black Parka might be waiting for her. She can always buy more clothes, a new bag. The only thing she regrets leaving behind is Michael's pages.

13

It has all the qualities of a dream, but Lily is awake. She's done this before. Used self-hypnosis to reach back and pull up this childhood memory. Aside from the pills, it's the only therapy she's applied to herself.

"You're counting back from a hundred," Lily says to herself, trying to block out the sounds of television and what may be the shrieks of lovemaking from outside her door in a cheap hotel near the Keleti train station. "When you get to one, you will be who you were that day. You'll remember."

Hypnosis can sometimes elicit new pieces of a memory from a witness. The trouble is, just like the witnesses she's seen it tried on, every time Lily has done it she's gotten a different version of events.

"One hundred . . . ninety-nine . . . ninety-eight . . ."

". . . three . . . two . . . one."

She's flying.

Her arms encircle the neck of a creature that pounds through the snow, the steam of its breath blown back against her face. She holds on tight but somehow knows she won't fall. She is tethered to the animal by a force as sure and unseen as gravity.

The cold wind makes it painful to open her eyes, and when she does it's only to catch a tear-jellied glimpse of the dark woods they pass through. The monochrome birches grow so close together she's certain the animal will knock into one and a branch will rip her from its back, but it never happens.

She travels further back into the memory now. Coming out of her room in the cabin sometime after the monster left. How she used dish towels and a bucket of snow to smear the blood around on the floor. Her mother's lifeless eyes wide open. The nostrils, forehead lines, lips—anything that could move was twisted as if by a funhouse mirror, inhuman and fierce.

Lily stood. Put on her boots and coat against the frigid air that now filled the cabin, its temperature the same as outside. She walked out with the idea of following the trail, but she's lost within minutes of entering the trees. The forest has crowded in around her. The icy crust atop the deep snow cuts into her thighs each time she plunges her feet forward. She hasn't gone far, but when she looks back the cabin is obscured from view. And now her fatigue washes over her. A tingling warmth she ought to resist, but how can she even begin to do that?

Hypothermia. Her mother had warned her about this, how the cold can seduce you into believing it's something else, the snow a warm bed you can lie down in.

Sleep.

The warmth curls its tail around her, whispering.

Sleep. Time . . . to go . . . to sleep . . .

She lies down even as she reminds herself that lying down will be the last thing she'll ever do.

. . . it's time . . .

There's something strong lifting her. Swinging her up by the ankles as she'd once seen a mailman do with the tied end of a sack of packages. Except the back she lands on is much broader than a man's.

She doesn't open her eyes. But when she thinks about it, she knows this is not a human being. It can't be. The thing in the cabin had stood on two legs. The creature gives her a second to wrap her arms around its neck before beginning to move.

Its speed builds so smoothly she doesn't notice how fast they're going until she blinks her eyes open and sees the snow-dappled trees flowing past, churning and cottony as the wake behind a ship. The animal rises and falls in jerks at once violent and predictable, galloping on four legs and then faster until she's sure they've launched into flight.

There must be a stretch of time when she falls asleep. Or maybe she simply can't remember how the animal comes to a stop and lays her on the ground. Yet that's where she ends up, sitting straight and feeling something biting her buttocks. She rolls onto her side and sees she's sitting on gravel at the side of a logging road that glows gray to the horizon.

Whatever carried her here is gone.

A hint of its presence remains in the cold air. But not something to see, not its smell. It takes the girl a while to identify it as a disembodied voice.

A pair of eyes come toward her, pale and enlarging. A truck's headlights. It slows when it spots her.

This is a distraction from her trying to remember what the voice had said. The thing that had saved her but had not arrived in time to save her mother.

The truck crunches to a stop in front of her. The driver's-side door opens and she hears country music. A man wearing heavy boots comes out.

"It wasn't a bear," the girl says before the man from the truck can hear her.

It was me, Lily. It's Michael's voice, whispering inside her head. *I came for you.*

The man from the truck stands over her. He says, "Jesus H. Christ." He says "cold" and "hospital."

I wasn't the monster. I didn't kill your mother.

The driver lifts her and puts her into his truck. She's curled up like a coil of rope, bathed in the warmth of Randy Travis on the radio and the burning air of the heater vents.

It was me. I was the horse.

14

After a night of little sleep spent fully clothed atop the polyester bedspread, Lily rises with the same thought tumbling around her head that she had when she lay down. Black Parka must be connected to Michael. And more than this too. Did the voice on the crank call she received before leaving New York belong to him?

She tries to think of the ways she might be wrong. Maybe Black Parka was one of those human traffickers she's read about, on the lookout for her "type." Maybe he was a thief who identified her as traveling alone, a thick clutch of euros in her pocket.

None of these alternatives stick. He was *hunting* her. And the look of him—his size, the intensity of his gaze—suggested a professional. The gun. An assassin.

The old Lily would be heading down the stairs of the shabby hotel now and hailing a taxi to the airport to take the next flight back to New York. But the old Lily wouldn't have found herself in a shabby hotel in Budapest to begin with. And the new Lily isn't going back. Not without the knife. Not without knowing what Michael knows about her mother.

She crosses the street and enters the station,

checking to make sure she hasn't been followed. The first train to the town of Eger leaves just after ten. From there, she can take a bus to the village of Szilvásvárad. Home of the Lipizzaner Horse Museum and stud farm. *Look into the horses' eyes.* Michael wants her to follow him, promising her a gift—of the knife? of knowing who her mother was? of himself?—and the only way she knows how is to pursue the story he tells. Szilvásvárad was where Dr. Eszes took Michael to be hidden. Where she hopes to hide while finding some new piece of him.

She buys a cheap knapsack and a fresh T-shirt, and drinks three espressos in quick succession served by a man who shakes his head at her as if she was refusing his advice each time. Once she's boarded, the train pulls away and she blinks out the window at the receding city, half expecting to see someone running after her.

Soon it's only countryside, with tiny cottages that want a coat of paint. In one of the yards a little girl watches the train pass. Straight dark hair and a severe expression even with her face at rest. She could be Lily at that age. When the elder Lily smiles and waves, the girl doesn't wave back.

Lily's childhood flashes as single words against her closed eyelids: orphan. Small. Alone. A narrative that embarrassed her with all its suggestions of Dickensian deprivation. While not happy years, she knows she's relatively lucky to have escaped the series of foster families without any particular scars aside from general neglect and the absence of anyone to put themselves forward as her primary guardian. As a result, she assigned her primary guardianship to herself. Her intelligence gave her what she needed to slip through most situations, excelling at school while managing not to attract the attention of the most toxic bullies.

Some people even liked her, boys and girls both, and she liked some of them back. But she had perfected the maneuvers that took her out of all candidacies for best friendship. She missed her mother with a permanent ache in the gnarled, twisting way a child grieves for the only parent it's ever known. But mixed with the sadness was the frustration of not knowing what it was Lily was sure her mother had intended to reveal to her. The cabin was a retreat from creditors, possibly the law, but it was also a place where her mother planned to teach her things.

"You have to be ready," Lily remembers her saying. "You've got to use what's in you and what you can take from others—take from me— and make it your own."

Lily disobeyed her mother once when she was told to stay in the cabin. Instead she'd followed her down the narrow path to the trailer. When Lily got there she found her mother lying on her back, looking at the sky. The position of her body suggested she'd been moving the moment before being spotted, as if she'd been not resting but rolling on the ground—or pulling herself out from under the trailer—a second earlier and had frozen at the sound of Lily's footfall.

"What are you looking at, momma?"

She turned her head to Lily. "I'm looking at you," her mother said.

Lily thought it was an odd thing to say—why would she have lowered herself to the ground just to look at her?—but she was used to her mother doing and saying odd things. She lay down next to her. The two of them in their secret place, watching the clouds turn into chickens and angels and bears.

Later, when she was on her own, Lily was never adopted, but transferred from home to home. There was always a reason to move on: the death of a foster parent, the realization that even a quiet child such as her was one child too many. And then there was the fact that with each passing year Lily became less adoptable. She recognized that her orphanhood made her someone who could be viewed as pitiable, the sort of person potentially corrected by the protections of love.

There have been those who offered that very thing, and each time they did Lily slipped away. It wasn't only their sympathy she found intolerable, it was the suggestion that intimacy or family or partnership was something she needed to get along in the world. She had resolved early on to demonstrate how professional competence and orderly habits were all one needed to pass as whole.

Excluding the police when she was six she had never told anyone that she'd seen her mother die at the hands of a real-life monster. It wasn't discretion that prevented her, but the fear that such a declaration would make her interesting. In her line of work, this was another way of saying there was something wrong with you.

She's the only one to get off the bus at Szilvásvárad.

It's colder up here in the hills, and Lily wraps her arms around herself. She's been left at the side of the road and has to guess which way to go. No other vehicles pass after five minutes of standing there. The only other life she can see is a rooster strutting in a circle in the backyard of a stucco house across from her. Eventually she decides on a direction she figures to be north.

Around the same bend the bus had taken there's a food truck in a gravel lot with an open window in the side. A woman with hands covered in flour appears. Though it's the last thing she needs, Lily points at the espresso machine. After the woman takes her money Lily asks where the horse museum is. When it's clear that not a word she's said has been understood, she mimics the neighing of a horse and drums her fingers on the counter to suggest a gallop. The woman laughs in Lily's face before pointing farther up the road.

Another quarter mile on there's a dirt lane heading to a stone manor just visible through the trees. The doctor's property is almost exactly as she pictured it: the house square with its door set in the center of its façade, a hill disappearing into the low clouds behind it. A plaque at the gate designates it as of historical interest. She can't read any of it except for a single word.

Eszes.

Lily knows that when she looks to the left she will see the stables up the slope. The sight of the building triggers the smell of hay and manure. There's a fence around the property and a booth at the gate where Lily guesses tickets can be purchased during the high season. But today the booth is empty, the gate open.

As she enters the stable the horses turn to look at her. Seven of them, all white. They watch her as if awaiting a command. The muscled flanks smooth as porcelain, the manes composed of visibly distinct hairs, each strand possessed of an internal glow. Lily has never seen animals as beautiful as these.

In all likelihood, this is where Michael had stood at some point as well. His appreciation of the horses' magnificence so great he incorporated them into his fantasy, making their blood his own. Lily can understand why. If she had to pretend to be descended from a species of animal, she'd choose the same one.

She approaches the closest stallion and it offers its head to be stroked. At the contact of her hand she senses a presence behind her.

"Michael?"

She turns and sees a caretaker in overalls and rubber boots, his face a red web of burst capillaries.

"Contessa," he says. "Hotel?"

For no other reason than it's two words she understands, she nods. "Yes, please. The Contessa Hotel."

That night, she rises from her bed and goes to the window.

As in a dream, he's there.

Sitting on a bench in the hotel's gardens. Even in the dark and from this distance she can detect the half-smile that shapes his mouth at the sight of her.

Go to him.

Lily remains where she is. The thinking part of her knows it isn't safe to be anywhere near him, yet that's what the deeper part of her wants. To hear his voice again. To feel if his skin is warm like the living, or cold like the dead.

Come.

132

Not her voice this time. His.

She rushes from the room without putting on her shoes so that her feet slap along on the marble floor. As far as she can tell, Lily is the only guest in the place. It lent a strangeness to every sound that echoed in the high-ceilinged, stone-floored lobby and hallways.

Outside, the cold hits her hard. But she doesn't go back. Rounds the corner of the building and down the grass slope to the garden.

He isn't on the bench. She scans the area, not believing he could have made it to the forest that borders the property in such a short time, but she can't see him. So she keeps going. As fast as she can through the meadow below the garden and toward the silhouette of the tree line, the high grass wiping its dewy stalks on her bare legs.

She stops at the edge of the trees. Behind her the orange windows of the hotel look as distant as a passing ocean liner viewed from the shore.

You've come too far, her voice says. *Nobody will hear you scream out here.*

From deep within the forest something moves through the leaves. What might be the flapping of wings. A single, yielding screech.

Lily backs away from the trees, stops when she turns to look up the slope to the garden.

He stands at the center of the organized flower beds where there was nothing a moment ago.

You're seeing things, psycho.

As if in reply, the figure beckons to her.

"I'm here," Lily whispers.

Then come, he says, his voice in her head, before starting away around the corner of the grand house and out of view.

Come.

15

The stable is heated by the breath of the animals who stare at her from their stalls, their hides pale as the two dimmed bulbs hanging from the rafters. Lily returns their hushed greeting with a bow she performs before she's aware of what she's doing.

The stallions look away from her to the far end of the stable where Michael stands.

"You must be cold," he says. "Come away from the door."

Lily approaches him, her bare feet shuffling over the straw on the concrete floor, and feels the temperature rise with each step she takes. She can't tell if it's from the collective heat of the animals' bodies or being closer to him. She stops when they're separated by the head of the last horse in the stalls. One of its liquid eyes on her, the other on him.

"I am so glad you had the chance to see them for yourself. The one you stroked today—that one there, beside you—belongs to the same bloodline that Dr. Eszes so dearly prized. I like to think that touch alone brings us closer."

"Is that why you've led me to this place?" she says. "To put my hand on a horse?"

"It is one piece of the puzzle, yes."

"Okay. I've done as you wanted. Now let me go."

"I'm not detaining you, Doctor."

"You're stalking me."

"You are mistaken," he says, his eyes black as the animals. "It is you who is following me."

He doesn't move closer but it feels as if he does. A growing cold within Lily that she guesses must be the part of her brain that's smarter than thought, the part that knows she's made a terrible mistake and that she'll be murdered here. It fills her with the heavy ice of fear, starting at her feet and moving up to her heart, closing her throat. But along with the terror there's also anger for believing in the instincts that brought her here, the judgment that promised he wouldn't hurt her. Instincts, she of all people ought to know, are what pull us from reason. Instincts get you killed.

"Why are we here?" Lily asks, working to swallow the cold spit in her mouth.

"You must have an idea."

"I'm asking you. Why are we here, Michael?"

He curls the corner of his lips to show that he's

not convinced by her attempt to be the doctor again, questioning her patient. His control is complete and she knows it. Yet there is something that turns his head away to gather his thoughts before returning his gaze upon her.

"This is the true meaning of blood," he says. "To look upon someone and see yourself."

"I look nothing like you."

"Perhaps not in appearance. But I recognize myself in you."

"A delusion."

"Is your solitude a delusion? Does it ever puzzle you why you have no real friends, no husband or lover?" he says, his lips stretching in what might be a smile of pity. "How do you reconcile your incapacity to love?"

She has to hide the fight required to pull the next breath into her chest. It's the surprise from what he's just said. The exact kind of questions Lily asks the lone wolf killers and isolated psychotics for a living, now being asked of her. And she has no answer for any of them.

He speaks again, changing the subject, before she can summon an unconvincing reply.

"You know there are people pursuing you?" he asks.

"There was a man in Budapest. But I lost him."

"He is one among many. And I very much doubt you have lost him for long."

"What do they want?"

"Me. So if they're after you, they are aware of our relationship."

"Relationship? That's not even close to the right word."

"What would the right word be?"

Lily can't answer this, so she works to return things to where she needs them to go if she is to remain alive into the next moment, and the next. Make this her story instead of his.

"Tell me about my mother," she says.

"In time."

"We're out of time."

"We have all night. And more, if we choose it."

He squints. A warning sign. *Don't push me.* Lily knows what he's capable of, but at the same time she remembers from her practical training that to survive an interaction like this, she can't allow herself to appear intimidated. It's crucial that some part of the authority she started out with at the Kirby be preserved by not wholly yielding to what he chooses to say and when.

He will try to make it a matter of the body, she recalls Dr. Edmundston advising her before her first solo interview with a client, a dismemberer. *You must keep it a matter of the mind.*

"You have to be careful," she hears Michael saying. "If they find you, tell them nothing. Delay them until I can come to you. If you fail in this, they will kill you. Do you understand?"

"Are they the police?"

"They are vigilantes," he answers. "A sophisticated version of the villagers carrying torches and pitchforks." He laughs a little at this, and the sound of it makes Lily start trembling, unable to stop.

She must resist him, maintain the boundary of *she* and *him*. She saw what he did to Dr. Edmundston, how calm he was, how sure. As calm and sure as he is now. It invites her to speak openly with him, be honest with him, confess whatever she's feeling so that those feelings might be understood.

"I want to go," she says.

"Are you afraid?"

"Of *course* I'm afraid!"

She didn't mean to admit to this. She meant instead to remind him that he's desperately ill, but it's over. She intends to go to the police, tell them he's set her up to look like a murderer. She'd lost track of that for a while, but she's not letting go of what's real again. Instead she only shouts aloud the only part of her thoughts she's certain to be true. She's afraid.

There's a silence between them. He blinks in regular intervals as if counting in his head, measuring her life against her death.

"Why are you doing this to me?" Lily says, and feels the tears race down her face, her throat so tight it's like speaking through a straw.

"Doing what? You're here because you came."

"Because I had no choice!"

He reaches into the pocket of his long coat. Pulls out something in a clear plastic bag.

"Here," he says. "Have your choice back."

Lily sees how the bag is dappled in blood, but it doesn't completely obscure her Henckel knife lying inside. She reaches out and takes the bag from him, holds it against her as if it's meant to keep her warm.

Michael takes a step back. It's her chance to go. But something holds her there.

"That was you, wasn't it, in the cellar of the old house yesterday," she says.

"My darling daughter, I am so grateful you made it to that place. However off-putting the circumstances, it makes me feel like a proper father for the first time. The patriarch delivering his offspring to view his birthplace! A rite of passage for both of us."

Michael raises his hand level with his chest and Lily looks behind her to see all seven stallions bow their heads.

"Never seen horses do that before," she says.

"That's precisely what Dr. Eszes's groomsman said when he saw them do it," Michael says, laughing. "He decided to hate me from that very moment. He was a hateful man by nature. A trait I would otherwise be indifferent to if he didn't sometimes take out his frustrations on the horses. When the tail struck their hides I could feel it myself. The horses' rage instantly mine as well."

The warmth of being near him brings another chill through Lily, one that lingers at the top of her head like a colony of spiders spreading through her hair.

"What was it like?" she asks. "Once the doctor brought you here?"

He considers her question, seeing the attempt to distract him for what it is. But his pleasure at the two of them being here, alone, plays out over his face, winning over the stony irritation at her playing games with him.

"Come," he says, pushing open the gate to the empty stall next to him. "We cannot stand like this all night."

Lily steps in and sits with her back against the wall in the corner, her body settling into the straw. Michael chooses the corner opposite hers, but he doesn't sit, only crouches. It enables him to keep his eye on her as well as the stable doors.

"I was assigned chores, and performed them for the first few days," he begins. "But soon I grew hungry, the jars of Lipizzaner blood only sipped at. It sickened me to ingest from animals, particularly these white stallions who were as close to brothers as I would ever know."

"Weren't you happy to be free?"

"I wasn't free. Not yet. But I loved to ride. I required no lessons, not that any were offered to me. The groomsman was against my riding, but he soon feared me even more than the doctor, who kept to the main house, the door locked. In the space of a single week the roles of all lodged there had been flipped, so that although I held the lowest position, it was clear I would do as I pleased. And what pleased me was to feed."

He lowers himself onto his knees and comes toward her. Lily doesn't move other than to press her back harder against the stone. There's the worry that even a flinch of apprehension might trigger attack, so she focuses on him, the man now stopping to kneel an arm's length from her.

"When did you start?"

She has asked the same thing of at least a dozen serial murderers before now, but this time she hears an intimacy in her question, a personal interest distinct from completing a diagnostic assessment.

"I will never forget riding into Eger one night and tying my horse to a tree in the square," he answers. "How brilliant my stallion looked in the darkness! There was a music academy there, the same one that's there today. Even in the November damp the windows were parted, expelling a symphony of lessons out into the night: piano, flute, violin. And a voice singing an aria. Mozart's 'Un moto di gioia mi sento.' It wasn't the perfection of the performance that moved me, it was the sad beauty of it, the way it lamented life's brevity even as it celebrated the joy of living. It opened a door in me. It was the music of my first killing."

He closes his eyes. Savoring the memory of the sound, the night. Then the recollection of violence opens his eyes again, glinting and darker than the moment before.

"Who?"

"A chambermaid," he answers. "Walking along the banks of the river. I followed her, filled with heat and sweetness. This was my poetry and I knew it. The hunt. The anticipation of the flesh a music of its own. She heard the steps approaching behind her and I could feel her thinking through her options—run, shout for help, face whoever followed her—and decide on doing nothing. I have since become used to this course of nonaction, but at the time it surprised me that the girl would let her end come so easily. It prompted me to speak to her. A friendly voice, asking directions to the town square. That is when she turned. Not that she believed me to be merely a lost visitor, but because it was how she was trained, how all civilized people are trained.

"Her skin. I remember that perhaps above all. How it glowed in the dimness of a quarter moon. The roar of blood through her veins like a waterfall. As she spoke to me she smiled, because I spoke to her as well—something about having traveled far and being in search of an inn for the night—and she thought the moment of danger had passed. She made a joke, a remark about the bedbugs at the inn and how they made a breakfast of you before you had a chance to breakfast yourself, and as I laughed—as we both laughed—I leapt."

Michael's hand drifts up toward her. There's no point in trying to get away, so Lily stiffens even more, a wooden doll awaiting his touch.

"I hadn't yet forged my steel teeth, and I was excited and awkward as a virgin, which in a way I was," he goes on. "Suffice it to say the business was messier and louder than the ideal. But it was a Hungarian town—people minded their own business. Eger had been traded between feudal leaders and crusading soldiers over and over. These weren't the first screams they'd heard in the night. And in any case the girl quieted once I started to feed in earnest—the normal calming submission of shock, I would come to learn— but I could feel the terror in her body like the fluttering heart of a sparrow. I pulled away from her throat and spoke to her. *Nem lesz több fájdalom, ígérem.*"

"What does it mean?"

"*There will be no more pain, I promise you.* I meant that there would be no more grappling and biting and tearing, but as soon as I'd spoken I heard the second interpretation of my words. We both did. *No more pain of this life.* She'd had her share. I could taste it—the character of her blood a far more telling thing than any sommelier can read from a vintage—and knew she'd been hurt, heartbroken. Which is not to say she was pleased to be in my arms by the soggy banks of the Eger-patak as her pulse slowed to nothing. But there was, I believe, a degree of relief. It would be like a student, poorly prepared, being told she would not have to sit for the examination she'd been dreading. There would be no more exams, ever."

His fingers stroke her cheek.

Out, out, out, Lily's inner voice tells her. *You have to get out.*

There's a look on his face that could be grief, the rising of buried regret. It gives her the sense that she might find an opening for escape if she uses the right words, the right tone. But as soon as she's spoken she sees she's mistaken.

"Did you know it was wrong?" she asks.

Michael pulls his hand away from her face and clutches a fistful of straw, slowly crushing it between his fingers.

"It was no more wrong than wringing a chicken's throat," he says. "Your *right* and *wrong* are the instruments of judges and priests, blunt tools used to build cages. But you and I—we choose freedom, don't we?"

He inches closer and a new wave of fear comes over her. Lily speaks to hold him in place.

"What did you do?" she asks. "Once you were done."

"By the time I had ridden back to the doctor's house it was almost dawn and my hunger was already returning," he says, sitting again, close enough now she can feel his warm breath. "The chambermaid had shown me not only the life ahead for me, but how feeding on human blood made me even stronger than I was before. I was drunk on the notion of my own greatness. And as it is with drunks, I only wanted more to drink."

"She wasn't the only one that night, was she?"

"No. When I returned the stallion to his paddock and started to my room, the groomsman stopped me. He began to chastise me for taking out a horse without his permission. And then I suppose he saw the blood on my face. He tried to close the door but I was faster now too. It felt as though I had all the time in the world to raise my hand, stop the door. Time to decide how to kill him. It would have been with my teeth if I hadn't known him to be the ignorant filth he was. So it was that I took his head in my hands, holding him as if to bring him closer for a kiss. Instead, I snapped his spine. He was dead then, but I didn't stop. I wrenched at him until his head was free. And then I threw his skull and heard it knock against the trunk of an oak in the darkness."

Out, out, out. Get out!

The voice inside Lily is little more than a smothered whisper.

"It wasn't as I had planned it. But it was

happening now," he says. "The end of my brief performance as a man. I knew that whatever followed from that moment would be my true life. I walked down toward the doctor's house with a single word repeating through my mind. *Gyilkosság, gyilkosság, gyilkosság. Murder, murder, murder.* It sounded to me like a question and an answer and a reason. The only word I needed. Eszes had closed the shutters on his main-floor windows but it was no trouble to smash one open with my fist. The glass cut me. A gash from wrist to elbow. But there was no pain. It felt like nothing more than a feather being drawn down the length of my arm. Even as I heaved myself onto the windowsill I could feel the tingling healing of the wound, the sides of the cut fusing together. By the time I made my way to the bottom of the stairs and heard the doctor shouting at his wife and son to stay in their rooms the blood on my arm was already dry."

"He knew it was you."

"I wouldn't have been surprised if he'd been up all night, waiting for me to come. Which meant I should have anticipated the rifle. The doctor stood at the top of the stairs with it aimed at me. He was wearing a nightshirt, I remember. One that revealed the blue-veined calves of his legs, the kneecaps soft as boiled eggs. I told him to put it down and he said no, even as he lowered the barrel until the gun hung loose in his arms.

'On the floor,' I ordered him, and again he said no, but nevertheless bent to place the rifle on the landing. A part of me wanted to ask him one last time what elixir he discovered that conquered death. But I made my way to the top of the stairs and looked into the doctor's face and saw for the first time that he didn't know the secret himself. It's why he hadn't told me. He had used a combination of ingredients and now he didn't precisely recall the recipe. I wasn't only alone. I was an accident. 'My wife. Son,' he whispered. I held him steady with my hands as I tore into his throat. His blood tasted old compared to the chambermaid's. The mustiness of corked wine."

Lily feels the color drain from her face and sees Michael cock his head in acknowledgment of it.

"No doubt the question of pity is now entering your evaluation," he says. "Hadn't I taken enough life for one night? And I might agree with you in hindsight. But you must understand that I'm not always what I seem. There are at least two versions of myself: the one who relates this account for you now, and the other who is an unstoppable cacophony of wants. The id, the subconscious, the demonic. Naming it makes no difference. It sings its own song and carries on until it is done."

"It was that part of you that murdered that man's family."

"Well done, Doctor! Shall I tell you how it

went? Eszes's wife was in her bed. When she saw me enter, dripping in her husband's blood, she sighed. It was the sound of her horror, of course, though it had the same breathy tenor of erotic expectation. It made up my mind for me. I would consume Mrs. Eszes until I'd had my fill. Afterward, I nearly forgot about the boy. I found him hiding behind the wardrobe in his room. A comical look-alike of his father, the narrow features and arrogant mouth. But his tears struck me as innocent tears. It was my first night of killing. I figured I ought to have exceptions to who I would feed on. Children, for one. I bent close to the boy. 'I am your brother,' I said, and left his room, pushing his father's body aside to make my way down the stairs and out the front door into the dawn light. All this before I changed my mind and returned. If it might color your judgment, know that I made it go fast."

He pauses and, from the stable's silence, Lily realizes the horses have been as transfixed by his voice as she has been. They wait for him to continue, and though his story has frightened her—the way so many of the events were described as happening *here*—she waits too.

Michael doesn't move. She parts her lips to speak but he raises his hand. A look of strange alertness alters his features so completely he appears a different person altogether. Or not a person at all.

He moves toward her on hands and knees and stops when his mouth hovers an inch from her ear.

"There's something out there," he whispers.

She listens for it but there's only the anticipation of what he will say or do next that starts a ringing in her head.

"Stay where you are," he says.

He doesn't touch her but she knows that he will, and this thought, instead of alarming her, washes her in heavy cascades of sleep. She resists it at first—no one knows she's here, she will never open her eyes again if she closes them now—but it's beyond her. The darkness comes upon her like the collapsing walls of a tunnel.

"Goodnight, Lily," he says, and kisses her cheek.

There's the single whinny of the horse in the stall next to them, a sound she understands as a warning, and then nothing.

16

S he dreams of blood.
A close view of busy cutting. It's impossible to blink, let alone look away. Something once alive is being severed, though she's too near it to identify its size, its species. The blade moves through it in a silvery blur of flesh.

The dream is so vivid it announces itself as not a dream at all but a memory returned. It's her own hand holding the knife. Not the Henckel from her kitchen in Manhattan but the one her mother used to skin and cut the animals she would hunt when they lived in the cabin in Alaska. Had she taught Lily to do the same, the places to enter the blade, the pressure required to separate hide from flesh? It's the sort of thing she might do, lending her daughter the knowledge to survive on nothing more than could be brought down with a small-gauge Remington in the woods.

She's skinning an animal but she can't pull far enough away to see what kind of animal it is. Something prevents her from viewing the entirety of what is laid out before her, as if her mind refuses it, admitting only sufficient information to carry out the next step, and the next.

There's a blink of darkness in which Lily drops the knife—she must have, as the knife is no longer in her hand—and she now holds a cloth.

The blood has soaked it through from her effort to clean the mess the animal has spilled. Lily goes back to trying to mop it up but only manages to spread it around like tar. This troubles her even more than the blood: she needs to make it go away. Her mother has taught her something a child should never be taught and now she wishes to be free of it. But that can only happen if she can clean up all the blood.

If it's only that, why are you so afraid? Lily's voice asks, reaching her even here in her subconscious. *Why do you want to wake up so bad you're trying to scream?*

And then she's awake. Screaming.

She's on her hotel room bed, lying atop the sheets, the chill of the room covering her like a stone lid. It's morning: a crack of gray between the slightly parted curtains. Her legs don't immediately respond to her wish to roll over and sit up, so she raises her head instead.

The knife, the voice within reminds her. *Where's the knife?*

She looks over and sees it there, still in the blood-spattered bag on the pillow next to hers. He must have brought her from the stable and laid her on the bed and placed it there while she dreamed.

Lily washes it in the bathroom sink, wraps it in a face cloth, and stuffs it in her backpack. Then she pulls the curtain wide enough to look out at the garden, meadow, and forest she'd walked to the night before. It's early enough that the sun has yet to burn off the fog that stays low to the ground. She's about to step away from the window when she notices the fog is not the only thing moving through the field.

A stallion stops to look up at her from the edge of the forest, its body whiter than the mist, so that it appears to be made of cloud. It's the Lipizzaner that occupied the stall next to Michael's and hers, the one that whinnied at the sound of approaching footfall.

Another horse joins it, then another. Soon six of them are gathered there.

There were seven in the stable, her voice tells her. *Where's the last one? The one you touched?*

Something close to panic seizes Lily.

It was him, she thinks, and is instantly certain of it. *It's how he got away. He rode the seventh horse.*

At the hotel's front desk there's a pair of policemen, one talking into his radio and the other looking out the door as if anxious to return to an activity outside he'll miss altogether if he stays here much longer. As she approaches the clerk at the desk Lily tells herself to appear calm. At the same time, it's clear something serious has happened and to pretend she hasn't noticed would call attention to herself as well.

"Everything okay?" she asks as she signs the credit card slip.

"There's been a murder, I'm afraid," he answers in formal English, the "I'm afraid" a mannerism that comes out bearing its literal meaning, as the man appears genuinely unsettled. And as Lily sees it in him, she is afraid too.

"Oh my God," she says. "Do they know who?"

"A man who worked at the stables," the clerk

says. Lily immediately remembers the man who greeted her yesterday, the one with a face of exploded blood vessels.

"The horses were set free," Lily says, feeling she has to say something but thinking of Michael, wondering how close he is.

The clerk looks at her strangely and is about to ask more when one of the police officers calls out to him.

Lily knows that if she doesn't move now she may never move again. She slips out the front door and walks the couple hundred yards down the lane toward the stables. The police are there in greater numbers. A van, three cars, an ambulance, all with roof lights ablaze. As she passes Lily notices a circle of officers off in the trees, a sheet-covered body at their feet.

When one of them turns to look her way she returns her gaze to the road. She expects them to call her back, but she makes it to the main road without interruption and finds the bench where she was dropped off the day before. She hears the bus coming around the bend before she sees it, and in the moment before it appears she takes the cloth-wrapped knife and buries it deep in the cigarette ash of a garbage drum.

17

That night, at dinner in her hotel overlooking the river and dome of Budapest's Parliament Building, Lily surprises herself by eating a large plate of roasted goose and potatoes. Even after she's finished she remains ravenous. Since she's met Michael she's feeling it more often. Not just a healthy appetite but an aching, low and constant within her.

You don't even know what that is, do you? her inner voice taunts her. *You're not hungry. You're horny.*

Instead of returning directly to her room she takes a stool at the lobby bar and orders a vodka soda. A celebration of sorts. She left her life behind to come to Europe all on her own and learned more than she wanted to know about an extraordinary patient. It almost got her killed, but she'd made it out. She won't linger, she won't make the same mistake again. There is only this night ahead of her in the four-star safety of the Hilton, and tomorrow she'll fly home. The knife is gone. Michael has no hold on her anymore. Until he's caught, she just has to mind her own business and wait.

The drink arrives and the alcohol warms her, drawing prickly sunshine through her chest and down the length of her arms. Her entire body alive with wanting.

"Bulls Blood."

A man has come to sit two seats away from her. He wears a suit, the tie loosened, end-of-day bristle along the ridge of his jaw. His eyes the pale blue of a malamute's.

"I'm sorry?"

"The wine." He points at the huge, upside-down glass bottle at the corner of the bar. "They call it Bulls Blood."

"Makes you strong. That the idea?"

"Not strong. Brave. Until the hangover, that is." He smiles and shows her his teeth. Perfect except for a small chip in one at the front, which only makes them more perfect. "My nerd name is Calvin. But I'm trying to be cool right now, so I'm Cal."

"Ellen," Lily says.

"Well, Ellen. Can a fellow American buy you a drink in return for ten minutes' conversation?"

Lily notes the absence of a wedding band on his ring finger. And more than this too. The laugh lines at the corners of his mouth, the pink flush of his lips. Something in his build that suggests the fitness that comes with contact sport over gym workouts. One of the martial arts maybe, or boxing. Lily's rational mind concedes that he's good-looking.

No, her inner thoughts correct her. *He's good in more than looks.*

She pulls her cell phone out of her pocket, finds the stopwatch app on the screen, and sets it.

"Ten minutes," she says. "Starting now."

"Okay. Well, let's see. I'm in medical equipment sales. Pitching MRIs and CT scans in order to update the hinterlands of Europe from bloodletting and witchcraft. Not the most exciting way to make a living but, believe it or not, I find it interesting. And I get to meet all sorts of people. Which circles me back to you. What brings you to Budapest?"

"I'm just a tourist. Taking in the history."

"It's off-season for that kind of thing. Maybe you haven't noticed how goddamn cold and wet it is?"

"I've noticed the discounts."

"Half-price goulash," he says, nodding in agreement. "Can't beat it."

They talk on about things back home, where they went to college, a debate over Chicago versus New York architecture. Just as the moment arrives when Lily decides she likes the way this man talks as much as the way he looks, the stopwatch on her phone beeps.

"Time's up," he says. "Do I get another ten if I buy another round?"

Lily buzzes with something more potent than alcohol. She looks at his hands, at once oversized and well-proportioned. She sees them in fists slamming into a punching bag. Sees them on her.

"Would you like to come up to my room?" she asks. She has no idea where this is coming from, but now that she's asked this question it's all she can think of, all she can feel.

He smiles and shows his chipped tooth again. "You know something, Ellen? I'd like that a lot."

She lets him in first before closing the door behind her and kissing him in the narrow entrance. He tastes as good as she hoped. And now his hands are sliding up her back, one holding her firm against him and the other dropping to her ass.

Instead of the bed he directs her toward the club chair in the corner, undresses her, then lets Lily do the same to him. The seat of the chair is set so low that when he sits his mouth is even with her belly. That's where he begins. His tongue traveling down, strong and warm.

"Come here," he says when she finally pulls away. His hands on her narrow hips, lifting her onto him. "Like that. Yes. Like *that*."

She thinks about Michael as she straddles the man in the chair. Her hands cover his face. With her fingers she sculpts Michael into existence, and once he's there, once it's him, she can't resist. She takes all of him.

• • •

After, Lily is thirsty.

The two of them lie naked on the bed, cooling the sweat from their skin. It's not water she wants, it's more vodka.

"I'll be back in a minute," she tells Cal.

She pulls on her shirt and pants and makes her way down to the bar. On the way she catches a red-cheeked glimpse of herself in a hallway mirror. She looks like Lily Dominick, but not like herself. An actor whose performance has demolished her reserve, leaving her at once sly and reckless.

That's not an actor, her inner voice counters. *That's you.*

At the bar she orders two vodkas then brings them back upstairs. The door to her room clicks shut behind her. That's when she notices the lights are off. She's sure they were on when she left.

"Cal?"

Lily steps through the little hallway and into the wider space of the room. There's a new smell that wasn't here before. The faint musk of horse hide.

The bedside lamp clicks on. It reveals two things to Lily in the same instant.

The first is Michael, an outline of blood around his lips. The second is Cal, spread out on the bed, his mouth lockjawed open in a silent scream.

Lily gags. It's what prevents a scream of her own from being voiced.

"May I?" Michael asks. He points his chin at the drink in her right hand. "Your friend won't need it."

He takes the glass from her hand, gulping the liquor down and running his tongue around his lips when he's finished.

Lily is trembling now, the sly and reckless actor abandoning her. It leaves her sickened by the dead body on the bed and terrified of his murderer, now standing almost within arm's reach in her room. More than anything what turns her stomach is how she'd imagined it was Michael she'd made love to in her mind, his body she'd brought into hers.

"You killed him!"

"You need to be more careful."

"Careful?"

"He was one of them."

Lily pulls her eyes from the dead man's body. "You're wrong," she says. "You're fucking insane."

"He was going to slit your throat." Michael bends and pulls a switchblade from the man's jacket pocket. Presses the release and the blade flicks out.

Lily backs away from him, putting her glass down on the bureau. Moments ago she was floating, a new power blooming within her. Now she's shaking and she can't stop.

"I'm finished," she says. "I'm going home."

"No. You're not."

"Because you won't let me?"

"Because you're halfway to learning an astonishing truth."

Lily feels like she's going to collapse. But she doesn't.

"You didn't come here for the knife. That's the rational thing you've told yourself, but it's not the real reason. You hope that, if you get some answers to fill the spaces within you, you'll be able to see yourself as whole for the first time in your life. To see if it works you need me to tell you about your mother, what I alone can impart to you. And I will, Lily. I promise I will. But first, you must understand who I am."

His words weaken and galvanize her at the same time. The same feeling she had when he'd recognized the inner absence within her when she'd stood before him in the stable in Szilvásvárad. *How do you reconcile your incapacity to love?* The disorientation that comes with hearing something about you, the truest thing, that until that moment has been kept hidden from yourself.

"What do I do?" she asks.

"You get away from here." Michael places the empty glass on the pillow next to the dead man's head. She watches it gently roll against his ear. "Before they find out you did this."

"But I *didn't!* You—"

"It's your room. Your image on the cameras in the bar. It's *you*. Because I was never here."

Lily wants only to disappear, but doesn't know how. "Where do I go?"

Michael rubs his eyes as if from a profound fatigue, but when he pulls his fingers away she sees the traces of blood he'd wiped from his lashes.

"I've left an address in your bag," he says. "There you'll find a man. His name is Eric Green. He will put to rest any remaining doubts you have about me."

It goes against reason—she's aware of this, tags it as such in her mind—but buried in her compulsion to escape is a desire to hold him. But then he speaks again and she catches the glint in his mouth.

"Don't disappoint me, Lily. We are on a path and we must keep to it or risk everything. Do as I say. Go now," he says, the metal teeth glowing. "Go!"

18

She has come here to retrieve some part of her mother. It's worth so much to her the threat of death hasn't stopped her, the meetings with a mass murderer, the voice within her reminding her what a fool she is. But is compulsion alone enough to explain why she's made these decisions?

What does *mother* mean to Lily?

It's a Dr. Lily sort of question. One she puts to herself.

She remembers her hair. More precisely, Lily remembers her mother brushing her hair, the long brushstrokes she counted out in the evenings no matter the shabby room they found themselves in or the absence of any witness to their dishevelment.

She remembers the singing. They must have been made-up songs, because Lily has never heard anything on the radio that she connected to the melodies her mother voiced. Ballads, lullabies. Music that Lily found comfort in, but also something unsettling, as if her mother's voice provided the soundtrack to her dreams, which invariably took unexpectedly frightening turns.

She remembers her mother's awful cooking.

It may have been the limitations of living on the road, grabbing whatever they could from convenience stores and truck stops, then the canned goods and gamey moose meat that sustained them at the cabin. Lily's body reacts to the very idea of the meals her mother made her eat. The steaming soups, always too spicy, too heavy with oil and flavors that tasted to her like weird mushrooms and pinecones. And the teas too. Homemade brews flavored with anise seeds and menthol and other powders and twigs that burned Lily's nose.

"Drink it," her mother would say, not forcing her but not letting her leave the cup full either. "It's good for you, honeysweet."

"It *stings*."

"That means it's doing what it's supposed to do."

"What's it supposed to do?"

Lily remembers her mother's arms pulling her close, the smoky smell of her sweater, the warm skin of her freckled throat.

Compared to Budapest, Geneva is a tidily organized city of pretty squares and identically sensible low-rise façades. Europe without the old bullet holes in the bricks.

5 Quai du Mont-Blanc. Geneva. Green.

This is the address Michael left in her knapsack. Where she didn't have to go but feels he would have punished her, or worse, if she hadn't. But her fear of him isn't the overriding reason she travels to Switzerland. She knows he's right: if she wants to learn what he can teach her about herself, she must keep to the path.

Before she walks the short distance to the

address from the Hotel d'Angleterre she decides to change herself. There's an undeniable thrill that comes with using the scissors she bought at the pharmacy to turn her pageboy into a spiky punk cut. She also calls down to the concierge and sends someone out to buy her a high-collared coat, makeup, sunglasses. Her intent is to discourage Black Parka or the police or anyone else from identifying her, but the truth is there's a pleasure in altering her appearance that has little to do with these practical concerns. There's power in changing yourself, and Lily feels it travel through her like the first tinglings of fever.

She approaches 5 Quai du Mont-Blanc by way of an alley. Once inside, she buzzes the name GREEN—606 on the tenants' list.

"Yes?" an older man's voice crackles at her from the speaker.

"My name is Lily Dominick. I've come to talk to you about Michael Eszes?"

"Those names mean nothing to me."

"What about the man who never ages. Does that ring a bell?"

There's a pause so long Lily is certain he will simply click off and leave her here. But then the inside door is buzzing and she pushes it open and starts up the stairs to the sixth floor.

She knocks and it takes some time for the man on the other side of the door to unlock it. When he finally opens it he scans Lily from head to toe and looks behind her to confirm she's alone before stepping to the side.

"Come in," he says. "Sit."

It's not easy. The whole apartment is stacked with record books, documents, binders, filing cabinets. A warren of paths lead from the door to the kitchen, the bathroom, a desk. Green is no taller than Lily, so that when he moves between the towers of printed material it makes her think of a child working through a labyrinth.

He props himself on the arm of a chair and Lily finds a stool stacked with old magazines. She moves them to the floor and sits.

Green looks at her intently through glasses in serious need of cleaning. "Who sent you?"

"I told you his name."

"Who are you working for?"

"No one. I'm a forensic psychiatrist with an unnamed client who escaped the facility where we were holding him. For reasons known only to him, he directed me here."

Green leans back and his chair yips at the strain. "What did he do?"

"Do?"

"If he was in a forensic psychiatric facility, I'm guessing he committed a crime."

"An assault."

"Details, please."

"He ripped the ears off a man."

"No one he knew?"

"A stranger."

Green looks around his desk for something and, when he finds a stained coffee mug, takes a sip of the dregs.

"Do you know who I am, Dr. Dominick? My vocation?"

"No."

"I'm a criminal investigator. A specialized one. In journalistic shorthand, I'm a Nazi hunter."

Lily crosses her arms. Uncrosses them. "I'm not sure I know why I'm here," she says.

"I do," he says. "The one who directed you here wants me to show you something."

"And will you show me?"

He ponders this a moment before rising. "I suppose you'll be safer if I do than if I don't. Either way, I hope you appreciate the danger you're in. Not to mention the danger you've brought upon me by being here."

"I'm sorry. I didn't—"

Green raises a hand to cut her off. He opens the drawers of one of the filing cabinets next to the window behind her, pulling out what look to be photo albums. Lands them on Lily's knees.

"The better part of my life's work has been spent finding war criminals and bringing them to trial," he says, sweeping a hand around the apartment to show the physical evidence of his labors. "Almost all the men and women we've identified have either been captured, imprisoned, or have died of natural causes. There is one, however, who is at large and remains something of a mystery to me."

"Because you haven't found him yet?"

"Not exactly," he says, and pauses, searching for the words. "Because I don't know what he is."

Green opens the top album on Lily's knee to a page marked a quarter way through. Taped to the paper is a photo, slightly blurred and poorly lit, as if taken in haste. A group of men in civilian trenchcoats and tweed jackets, most smoking, none smiling, about a dozen in all, and flanking them a pair of German officers in uniform. The men are arranged in two rows, none looking particularly pleased to have their picture taken. The room they stand in is mostly bare except for detailed maps on the wall and, through a window to the side, the spire of a church.

"What's this?" Lily asks.

"The only known photograph of a special unit assembled in Leipzig in April 1942. The German advancement had slowed and the Allied Forces, for the first time, were seeing genuine opportunities for counterattack. One of Berlin's responses was the creation of unorthodox approaches. Saboteurs, the bombing of non-military targets. And these men in the photo. Men who weren't recruited from the existing military ranks. Instead, they came from prisons, asylums.

They were given language training as required—French mostly, though some were intended to make their way to English soil—and put into the field."

"What was their assignment?"

"Demoralization. In some instances, they were tasked with the assassination of specific individuals, but others were left to their own inclination. Their job was to give another face to Nazi power. Not just superior military might as shown by their tanks and armies, but a capacity to strike innocents in their own homes."

As he speaks, Lily notices that Green is considerably older than she first thought. She'd guessed seventy at first, but would now add another decade. And along with his wrinkles, she can also see the rage in him. A darkening that builds behind the smudged lenses of his spectacles.

"So how does this relate to the man who sent me?"

Green taps the photo. Lily looks down and studies it again. And then she spots him. Michael. Standing in the second row, his face averted.

"It looks like him," Lily says. "But that isn't possible. This picture is over seventy years old. But the man I know . . . he looks exactly the same."

"Keep looking."

Lily flips the page and finds three other photos.

All of them taken with a telephoto lens so that, again, the images are less than crystal clear. But it appears to be him. Coming out of an office building, entering the Paris Métro, walking down a busy Tokyo street. Judging by the cars and cell phones, all the photos were taken in recent years.

"Franz Bachmeier. That was his name when he enlisted," Green says. "Of course, the name is meaningless, considering how many he's adopted over his life. My colleagues and I have been in pursuit of him for some time."

"Bachmeier," Lily says, trying the name out for herself. "Do you know what happened to him in the war?"

"We think he was deployed to Poland. But soon afterward, his record comes to an end."

"Then he must have been killed. And these other photos—they're another person. They must be."

"No. There is evidence that he was imprisoned soon after war broke out. Three years later he took the opportunity for freedom when it was offered to him. And then he did what he's best at. He disappeared."

"You say he might have been in prison. For what crime?"

"What do you think, Doctor?" Green says, closing the album and lifting it into his arms.

"Murder?" She says it tentatively, and he nods, then returns the album to the file drawer he got it from. He remains at a distance from Lily, the wan light from the window making him appear more blurred than the man in the photos.

"I have done what he wanted me to," he says. "And now I'm wondering why."

"I don't have the answer to that. He's obviously done a lot of work to support the fiction he's now unspooling for me. Some of that work involves committing terrible crimes. But people don't live to be two hundred years old, Mr. Green."

He combs the white wisps of his remaining hair with his fingers, a tic that might have been necessary when he was younger but now looks like a strange way of scratching his scalp.

"The Nazis enlisted some of the finest scientists of the age in pursuing experiments that wouldn't be permitted previously," Green says. "Many of them obscene. The pursuit of the supernatural. Immortality. Perhaps in this man they succeeded and didn't see it before he slipped out of their grasp."

"I don't doubt your authority in your area of expertise, Mr. Green. But my expertise would suggest a far more likely explanation. The man I've encountered is an extremely disturbed person who has built a world, an elaborate stage set, to fit his own mythology. As far as I know, he's compensated you—or perhaps threatened you—to show me these doctored photos as a way of supporting his tale. He's an extraordinary man, no question. But he can't be what he says he is."

Green is so still that Lily thinks his mind has wandered elsewhere. Then he takes a single step toward her before stopping, as if he can't stomach the very smell of her.

"This is not a practical joke, Dr. Dominick. I will forgive the offensiveness of your suggestion on the grounds that you are struggling with accepting what is plainly before you. But while I cannot explain what Bachmeier is, I know he exists, just as I know that evil exists. Do I need to present evidence of the latter to you as well?" He gestures both arms at all the stacked records and papers.

"I meant no offense. But you have to—"

"I would like you to go now, please."

He's already making his way to the door, unlocking the bolts and chains. Lily follows him and when the door is just wide enough for her to slip through he gestures for her to exit.

"I'm truly sorry," she says.

"Maybe you are. Maybe not. But I fear you will be soon."

She makes her way back to the hotel feeling unsettled and angry. At Michael, but mostly at herself. It distracts her enough that it takes a moment for Lily to notice the concierge rushing after her as she enters the lobby.

"Dr. Dominick?"

"Yes?"

"A message for you."

He hands Lily a small, blank envelope and then slips away. She opens it. Inside a card, a single word, in handwriting she now knows better than her own.

Diodati

19

She remembers the name from the author biography in her edition of *Frankenstein*. The villa on the shore of Lake Geneva where Mary Shelley got her idea for the novel that would make her famous.

Strengthened by a hot shower, Lily gets into the backseat of a taxi outside the Hotel d'Angleterre with a renewed grasp on the rational. There was an article she remembers reading that argued how everyone has their own doppelgänger in the world, a result not of the uncanny but simply the limited variations that can be applied to the human face and form. She tries to convince herself that Green's photos established nothing other than certain people can look alike if caught at the right angle.

You don't believe that, her inner voice scolds.

It was him. You know it was because you saw yourself in his face.

The taxi driver asks in French where she'd like to go.

"The Villa Diodati," she says.

It's a short drive. What may have taken an hour or more in the gloomy summer of 1816 when the Shelleys vacationed here requires only fifteen minutes by car. Lily asks the driver to wait for her and he takes a spot in a small parking lot down from the villa's front gate.

She walks along the roadside past high shrubs and trees carefully planted to hide the mansions and consulate offices on the other side. Lily recognizes the building before confirming the address on the stone gatepost: Diodati 9. Her Internet search told her the place had been converted into apartments and that visitors could come no closer than the curb, but it's enough for Lily to be here and see it for herself. Enough for what? To understand how someone like Michael imagined himself into being. Standing in a place where others were before you, a place where history was made, and inserting yourself as a direct link to that history. Mary, her poet husband Percy, the proto-celebrity Lord Byron were *here.* Just as she is now.

There's a grass slope next to the property where a single stone bench faces the water. Lily makes her way down by a worn path that may have been the same that Mary used to reach the lake, except today the path is cut off by the fences and hedgerows of other properties. She can glimpse the choppy water of Lac Léman through the bare branches, but can't get there from here.

When she turns to head back up, he's there, sitting on the stone bench. Staring at neither the villa nor the lake, but at her.

Lily walks as calmly as she can up to him, taking her time in the hope that someone else—a tourist, a gardener, her taxi driver—will join them, but they remain alone.

"Sit with me, Lily."

"What if I refuse?"

"Why would you?"

"You're a fugitive. A violent criminal. Psychotic. There's three reasons."

"Now think of the reasons you are here. If you're honest, you will see how they have little to do with my threats—not anymore. In any case, to deny me would trigger my anger, and you have already seen the outcome of that."

He pats the spot next to him on the bench. Lily sits, the stone hard under her thighs.

"Green showed me the photos," she says. "They don't prove anything."

"Do you hear yourself?"

Lily *does* hear herself. And it's the sound of the

last struggles of her mind against what she feels. What she knows.

He clasps his hand over hers. His touch is warm, the low hum of his energy, a sub-bass tingling. She can't move her hand away. Not that she tries.

"How did you know my mother?"

"We're almost there. Before her—my only wife—I need to speak of my first love."

He squeezes her hand tighter and it relaxes her, pulling her into his words like a tidal current.

"From the moment I saw Mary Shelley I wanted her to love me," he says. "Did she? Who can say? Authenticity of emotion is not my specialty. What is known is that I spared her life, and in return she took mine. For though she chose her anemic husband and an existence of inky struggle over me, she fashioned something from her betrayal. A book. A novel of gothic horror written in response to a contest proposed by Byron, a contest she decidedly won. The first masterpiece of the genre, one that is assumed to be about the dangers of science but will always for me be a kind of unrequited love letter."

Lily tries to imagine what this place would have looked like then but instead she clearly detects what it *felt* like. To be Mary Shelley, a teenaged girl meeting the man she sits next to now. It's ludicrous. Yet she feels the possibility of it in the grip of his hand.

"Later accounts describe her as beautiful, but this is inaccurate," he goes on. "Better to say she was English. Physical awkwardness combined with a compensating pride. And intelligence. A mind that somehow announced itself in the pigeon-toed stride, the sharp nose raised to the air, smelling for fresh metaphors. To me, Mary Shelley was an irresistible portrait of England itself."

"Is that why you came here? To see her?"

"Not at all. I came for a sighting of the celebrated Lord Byron, whose fame as a debauched monster I took a personal interest in. He was not difficult to find. Everyone in the cafés of Geneva was talking about his renting the Villa Diodati. I took a room at an inn across the lake, just there," Michael says, pointing through the trees. "The innkeepers recognized the advantage of being in such close proximity to the poet, so they set out telescopes to be hired by the half hour. Through them, one could spy on Byron's residence and wait to see the great man emerge, hopefully with a naked damsel or a scribbling quill in his hand. I first saw Mary Shelley through one of those lenses."

He sighs. A confrontation with buried emotion that surprises him even more than it does Lily.

"So you ended up staying for her."

"I stayed to find a purpose," he says, shifting to look directly at her. "By that summer, I had finally perfected my habits of killing. I had also observed how I didn't age the way men do, my face, my skin, everything the same as the day I was made. Such a gift! But one that brought new questions to mind: If I were to live forever, how would I spend the time? What of art, poetry, music? The answer lay across the lake. Through their genius, Percy Shelley and Lord Byron might be my brothers. Maybe they would be blind to the horrific in me and see the sublime. Yet if I was to be honest it was always the girl I thought of when I pictured the activities of the villa's residents. It was her imagination summoning me. You see, I'm not alone in reading minds. Mary Shelley could sense I was close to her, just as you can sense me close to you now."

Lily looks behind her to confirm they remain alone. It's not only the grassy patch that is unoccupied, but no sounds from the road or surrounding buildings reach them either. It's as if the world has been frozen for the time the two of them sit on the cold stone bench, their hands held.

"Over the next few days, I took to walking to the borders of the Diodati property, hiding in the vineyard rows you see there," he continues. "Mary had an infant with her, a son, so I had to wait to see if there was a time when she could be met on her own. I became impatient, my initial desire for conversation escalating to a desire to feed. One evening I went to the villa with the intention of entering the residence and taking her. I was making my way across the property's moonlit lawn"—he draws a finger through the air, showing his progress a hundred yards away—"when I felt a presence looking down at me from one of the second-floor windows."

"It was her," Lily says.

"She carried no candle but the moon was enough to color her outline, her hair down, the long English fingers clamped to the frame as if to hold her straight. I wore my steel teeth and hands, and wondered if she could see them in the dimness. She indulged her curiosity by staring. And I stared back. It was the first time I'd allowed anyone to observe me plainly in that way in the middle of the hunt. The exposure aroused me. You may think me foolish, but I thought it was romance."

He's getting this from research, a part of her old self tries to tell her. *Biographies, criticism. He's making it up.*

Lily knows this is the conclusion she ought to be holding on to, but can't help hearing something familiar about the story he tells that has nothing to do with its connection to a famous book. It's as though she's possessed a hazy, fragmented knowledge of it since birth, as they say it is with reincarnated souls who recall details from their previous lives.

"What did you do?" she asks.

"There was an interruption—a dog's barking, as I recall—and I turned away, retreated into the darkness, feeling her eyes on my back with such an intensity it was as if I were a poem and she was memorizing me. Later, she would write of this moment in disguised terms."

Michael tilts his head back and recites the written lines from memory.

" '. . . the artist . . . He sleeps, but he is awakened; he opens his eyes; behold the horrid thing stands at his bedside, opening his curtains, and looking on him with yellow, watery, but speculative eyes.' "

"Mary wrote that?"

"Yes."

"I don't remember it from the novel."

"It's from her original introduction. A recounting of a dream in which she is the artist. And I am the 'horrid thing.' Of course I didn't know about any of that as I slipped away and returned to my inn. All I knew is that I would never again let myself wish to feed upon the woman at the window. All I wanted was to woo her."

Michael squints into trees down the slope in front of him, searching for a spot along the shoreline.

"There used to be a trail that followed the lake and I was there two mornings later, putting my clothes back on after a swim when she came upon me," he says. "She introduced herself only as Mary. We spoke of what brought us to Lac Léman. I said I was a scholar of Hungarian folktales taking his sabbatical leave from the university. When I asked why she walked alone she said she liked to go for hikes ever since her parents sent her to a remote corner of Scotland when she was a girl. The solitude and closeness to nature assisted her in what she called her 'waking dreams.'

" 'I can assure you I am no dream,' I said, and immediately regretted the obvious flirtation. But either she didn't notice, or she appreciated it, because it only seemed to warm her attentions. 'Tell me about yourself. I like nothing more than stories,' she said, and sat herself down a few feet off the trail in the grass. It may not seem remarkable to you, Lily, but it was a bold thing she did then—to sit a few feet away from a stranger and invite him to tell her a tale."

"You volunteered everything to her?" Lily asks, surprised by the note of jealousy in her voice.

"Not at first. I told her my name was Michael. She spoke of the 'men in the house' who stayed up late, drinking and criticizing the latest literary works published in London, a subject she was capable of speaking to but couldn't because she would be sent off to tend to the child in the nursery. I don't recall much about what else we spoke of at that first meeting. My memory is more attached to the way she looked at me. It was impossible to tell if she suspected I was the figure she'd seen outside her window a couple of nights before, though she considered my face in a way that suggested she did. Maybe this was only her writerly self, capturing details to be recorded later on the page. Being a fool in such matters, I wanted to believe that she looked at me that way because she was falling in love."

Lily is suddenly aware of how she is looking at him. Would it be love that Michael would see there too? If he did, would he be entirely mistaken?

"What did she do?" Lily asks, realizing she's curious to know if she will do the same thing, whatever it is.

"Nothing. It is what I did that matters. Because before she could stand, I leaned over and kissed her. She neither reciprocated nor pulled away. If anything, she seemed to savor the taste of my lips. I asked if I could see her the next day. 'Well you may, if you be here and I go walking again,' she said, her cheeks colored by two perfect crimson circles. 'I have the most remarkable story I'd like to tell you,' I said. 'Something I've never told anyone. Occurrences which are usually deemed marvelous.' She nodded at this. And then, without another word, she got up and proceeded along the trail, around a corner of the shore, and disappeared."

"You've told me why you're sharing your story with me," Lily says, pulling away from him in resistance to the urge to lean closer. "But why share it with her?"

"Because I wanted my lover—my imagined lover—to be the one to draw my portrait in words," he replies after a moment of consideration. "Would she see a man or a monster? For all three of the writers I ended up revealing myself to it was never what I wished to see. It's why I stopped pursuing them. And why I found you."

Lily feels a heat in her throat, her cheeks, and realizes she's blushing. She'd turn away but it would only highlight it more, so she holds herself still and waits for him to continue.

"There was another reason I shared myself with Mary Shelley," he says. "The competition I wanted her to win. 'Byron has presented us with a challenge,' Mary told me the next morning when we met by the lake. By then I confessed that I knew who she was, and who lived in the villa. 'We will each write a ghost story. But I am bereft of an idea,' Mary said, and smiled at me. 'Oh, Michael. What shall I write about?' I said she ought to write about me. It was out before I could prevent it, though I have little doubt she would have used the details I had already related to her. She was educated, talented, and possessed of an uncanny imagination. But more than this, Mary was ambitious.

"We kissed again, there in the grass. It was to be for the second, and last, time, and I think part of me knew it. 'You promised a story,' she said once we had broken from our embrace. I told her I was not what I appeared to be. I told her I was not a man. Not a human being in any sense that mattered. She leaned away from me, but not in fear. Mary Shelley had traveled here in the name of discovering the strange and remarkable, the sort of things I called 'occurrences which are usually deemed marvelous,' and precisely how she would word it in the novel I was moments from giving life to, giving to her. 'If not a man, then what are you?' she asked."

Michael shifts on the bench as if he's about to rise, and Lily experiences a bubble of grief at the prospect of him releasing her hand. Instead, he stays seated, grips her hand even tighter.

"Isn't it funny, Lily, how this phrasing echoes yours at our first meeting? And just as with you, I told Mary the truth. When I was finished I expected her to ask any number of questions. I supposed she took me for a madman. But though it may only be a lover's hubris, I prefer to believe she accepted all of it as true. It's why Mary's book has such resonance. I said how I hoped she would now win her ghost story contest. 'Oh, I think we can put all this to better purpose,' she said. I remember that 'we.' Did she mean herself and her husband, whom critics would later assume had written the book? Or did she mean me?"

His grip on Lily's hand comes close to hurting—then it *is* hurting—but she looks at his face, sees the new and disfiguring anger in him.

"There would be no *Frankenstein* without me," he says. "Instead of me feeding on her blood, it was she who was fed. This girl devoured my life and created another monster, part of it made from me, and part of it her own gothic dreaming. Even her husband was surprised by the story and where it could have come from, 'as every cuckold is surprised.'"

He releases her hand. The air is colder than a moment ago, jetliners leaving criss-crossed contrails in the sky, the sound of a delivery truck struggling along the road behind them.

"You walk up the hill and I will walk down," he says, already standing.

"Wait. I need to—"

"Don't look back. Keep moving. And this," he says, placing a DVD in a plastic sleeve next to her. "This is for you."

He walks away. His gait unhurried, yet he covers the ground between the stone bench and the tree line in a quarter of the time it took Lily when she first arrived. Somehow he finds a way through the hedgerow, or a gap in the fence, because he's there one moment and swallowed by shade the next.

She walks back toward the parking lot the same way she came. The taxi is where she left it, the driver turning the key in the ignition when he spots her.

"Did you see him?" the driver asks when she slides into the backseat.

"See who?"

"Frankenstein," he says with a snort of laughter before pulling out of the lot.

20

The taxi drops her off in front of her hotel but she doesn't go inside. Instead she carries on another block to Eric Green's building. Lily knows that if she needs to convince anyone else of the impossible history that she's contemplating about Michael—convince them that she's not the crazy one for believing there may be some strand of truth sewn into his fabrications—she'll need as much evidence as she can, and Green's wartime photo is all there is.

This time, both the outer and inner security doors are open. As is the door to Green's apartment. Lily nudges it wider with her elbow, careful not to touch any surface with her hands, and steps into the maze of stacked books and documents.

She finds him on the floor. Lying on his back, eyes closed behind his smudged lenses, arms outstretched, as if carried and placed there while asleep. The two puncture marks in his neck and the blood haloed around his head the only indications that he'll never wake up.

He lies in front of the filing cabinet he took the photo albums out of.

It's foolish to stay any longer. But she has to be certain.

Lily steps around Green's body, careful not to let any part of her foot touch the still spreading perimeter of blood. The drawers have been left open. She looks inside. The album containing the Bachmeier photos is gone.

Before today, either Michael had found her, or he'd given her explicit instructions where he could be found. Now it's up to her. He said it was a path they were on, but Lily recognizes it now as something closer to a course of study, an escalating series of lessons and tests. All having to do with coming to think as he thinks, and feel as he feels.

If she's right, why submit to it? What's in it for her to think and feel as he does?

Because it's the only way to know what he knows.

It's why she's in the Geneva airport booking a ticket to London. Every remaining direction of his story that she knows of leads there. The city where Bram Stoker lived most of his life.

But that's not the only reason she's chosen the English capital. There's a silent communication between Michael and her now that confirms it. Is he reading her mind or is she reading his? All she's certain of is that she can feel him inside her, the presence of his thoughts commingling with her own.

She's seeing how far this connection between them goes, legs crossed on a leather bench in the departure lounge with her eyes closed, feeling for him, when she's aware of someone sitting directly across from her. There was ample room on either side a moment ago. Which keeps Lily's eyes closed.

"Dr. Dominick?"

Lily recognizes the voice. The crank call she got in New York. *You're not safe.* The voice she imagined belonging to someone well-built, handsome. Then she opens her eyes and sees a monster.

It's his face. The nose not quite where it ought to be. One of his cheeks—on the same side as the other damaged parts, so that a rough line separates the *before* and *after* of his features— mapped by scars.

"I didn't mean to startle you," the man says,

then raises a hand to point at his face. "Not much I can do about it."

"You called me. In New York."

"Correct. I guess, in your line of work—"

"Who are you?"

Lily looks past him, searching for a policeman to wave down, her legs rigid.

"Please don't try to run. It'll only—"

"Stay away from me."

"There's no need to be afraid. I'm not going to hurt you. In fact I'm here to make sure—"

"Tell me who you are or I'll scream."

"My name is Will," he says. "Will Muldover."

"How do you know who I am?"

"I work for a government agency. A special operation."

"What government?"

"The US government, of course. Who else hires goons like me to do this kind of shit?"

Lily looks over his shoulder and reminds herself to be comforted by the presence of fellow travelers, the phone gazers and luggage pullers all close by yet out of earshot.

"You're CIA?"

"I suppose so, sure." He shrugs. "You wouldn't believe how complicated the lines between these things can get. Officially, I'm a consultant. Totally off the books."

"Like an assassin. They pay you to take people out? Someone like me?"

"If I was here to take you out you'd be dead by now." He draws his hand over the stubble of the unscarred side of his face, a *Where do I begin?* gesture. If he's concerned she's going to dash down the terminal's hall, he doesn't show it.

"We're looking for someone," he begins. "He goes by various aliases, but you would've known him by his client number when you interviewed him at the Kirby. After his escape, you traveled to Hungary either under his instruction or in search of him yourself. Am I right so far?"

Should she admit to knowing what he's talking about or deny it? She can't decide, so says nothing at all.

He leans forward, propping his elbows on his knees. It's meant to shrink his size, to relax her, and while it works, Lily tells herself to fight it. This is the moment she's been warned about. Will Muldover—if that's his real name—may or may not kill her here and now, but what's certain is if she mishandles this, Michael definitely will.

"I'm guessing you've recognized some of his extraordinary capacities and you're curious. Who wouldn't be?" he says. "My predecessors have been tracking him for some time. As far as we know, he's the only one in the world of his kind."

"What kind is that?"

"I'm not sure it has a name. I guess 'immortal' will have to do."

Lily makes a series of instant mental notes.

First, this man is apparently confirming Michael's claims to be over two hundred years old, which either makes it true (which is impossible) or shows she's being played with (which is entirely possible). Second, he hasn't mentioned her mother or Michael's beliefs about her parentage, which means he's either holding on to that or doesn't know.

"I don't have to tell you anything," she says.

"But you *should* tell me."

"Why?"

"I work for the good guys," he says, as if it's as simple as that. "This individual has brutally killed thousands of people. Because he isn't human and because he's been alive three times as long as people usually live, he doesn't exist in any official sense. No national or international police organization is looking for him. There's only me and the other guys."

"What other guys?"

"The ones tracking you. Maybe you've noticed them? They're on the opposite team. But they want the same thing I do."

"Which is?"

"Him."

Lily thinks of Cal's drained body in the bed they shared in Budapest. The man in the black parka who'd chased her from the square.

"I still don't know what you're talking about," Lily attempts.

"You're lying."

"Yeah?"

"Yeah. See, I'm trained in recognizing the tells in people."

"How's that?"

"For one thing you look like you're about to puke."

He's right. She fights to bring in a breath and hold it down until her stomach settles.

"The person you interviewed at the Kirby was briefly incarcerated some years ago," Will continues. "Caught by a pair of highway patrolmen ditching a body off a bridge in Louisiana. Once we became aware of his capture, we told the prison doctor to take a blood sample before we flew down to pick him up. It's a good thing we did. Because as the sample was being taken, he extracted considerably more blood from the doctor than was extracted from him. And then he was gone."

"But you still had his blood."

"That's right. And our lab ran every test there is on it. The results were mostly normal. But some of it demonstrated extraordinary characteristics. I'm not a scientist, but from what I understand it's like a superpowered antioxidant, cells that demonstrated resilience to all manner of disease. The reversal of advanced cancers in rats. A medical game changer, to say the very fucking least."

Three weeks ago—three days ago—Lily would have found this stranger's account preposterous, the sort of claim she'd hear babbled by a lunatic in one of the Kirby's interview rooms. Yet whether it's the more fantastical tales she's entertained since, or how it would explain so much of what she couldn't explain before, either way it enters her with the solid weight of the truth.

"So why not make the medicines and save the world?" she asks.

"We'd like to. But we need him."

"You mean his blood."

"Yes. His blood."

Lily thinks of Michael outside somewhere in the night, hunting. But if Will is right, if he's telling the truth, the one who's brought so much suffering to so many has the capacity of ending the suffering for millions more. She struggles to hold these competing possibilities straight in her head.

"What about the others? Are they after the same thing?"

"We're not exactly sure. But it's not to help anybody other than themselves. We know they have considerable resources, possibly even greater than ours. And we know they've killed many innocent people in their pursuit of him. They're a collection of soldiers, torturers, hit men. The best at their particular skills."

"I can't help you."

"Listen to me, Lily. This individual—he's good at many things, lying being one of them," Will says. "He can get into your head. I don't know how he does it, but he can. Maybe you think he's your friend. Maybe you're even a little in love with him. But he will eventually rip you open the same as everyone else he comes across. It may be that he thinks he can stop himself. Except he can't."

He slides to the very edge of the seat so that Lily can smell the soap he showered with. While she recognizes that she should be repulsed by him, she finds herself resisting the urge to bring her fingers up to his ruined face. Sympathy can lead to attraction too, Lily realizes. It aroused something other than passion but something related nevertheless, the desire to connect, to show someone they aren't alone and in so doing, show that you aren't either.

"He's killed children," the man says. "Hundreds of them. And he'll never give up."

Lily expects him to wait for a revision of her refusal to assist him but instead he stands. He's taller than she would have guessed. He searches in his jacket and hands her a card. Lily glances at it. A number with a New York area code.

"That's a call-me-anytime offer. Don't wait too long to use it, because here's the truth: I'm your only chance of getting through this alive."

His hand comes up and for a moment she

expects him to put it to her skin, to squeeze the top of her exposed shoulder or stroke a stray lick of hair behind her ear, but he only slips it into his pocket. He moves away from her and joins the flow of passengers heading to their gates.

When he's completely out of view Lily studies the number on the card before ripping it up and letting the bits of paper fall on the carpet at her feet like snow.

21

At Heathrow she takes the tube into the city, emerging at the Russell Square station to look for a hotel. It has to be a good one, because she figures only those places could arrange for a DVD player to be brought to her room. She goes on for a block before deciding on the Montague, where the concierge says he'll have one sent up within the hour.

Instead of waiting, Lily heads out to buy some clean underwear and socks. Once she finds Oxford Street she gets swept along by the crowds, the pounding club music from souvenir shops, and the roar of buses pushing the traffic along next to her. On a wall of TVs in a store's window display the news is reporting the disappearance of a twelve-year-old boy on his way to school, his photo that of a cherry-cheeked kid with jug ears wearing a Spurs jersey. It supplies Lily with almost enough everyday noise and horror to stop her from thinking about being followed. Not just by Michael now, but by the twisted-faced Will, as well as the unnamed ones who will use her before killing her. So far as she knows, all of them bad guys.

When Lily returns to Russell Square it's dark. Despite the cold, men and women stand outside the pubs drinking, and part of her wants to be with them. One of the men, good-looking and tipsy, steps away from the others and waves. "C'mon! One on me, luv!" he calls to her, and he clownishly frowns when she shakes her head and walks on.

Once in her room she sees that the disc player has been set up as she asked. Lily opens the DVD case and, along with the disc, pulls out a tightly folded square of delicate paper, yellowed with age, their surfaces spiderwebbed by Michael's handwriting.

Lily decides to watch the DVD first. Takes a shuddering breath. Presses play.

It's her mother.

Judging by the saturated colors and slightly flickering frame, the footage was shot on film, a Super 8 or something like it, then later transferred to video. The effect is to authenticate that it's her, unquestionably the past. She sits on a tartan sofa in what, judging from the faded print of flowers in a vase on the paneled wall behind her, is a cheap motel room. Her hair wet, clothed in a ratty white bathrobe. She looks tired, but summons a smile.

"Let's see the little worm," a man's voice says from behind the camera. "The little Worm Princess."

Michael's voice.

The camera comes in closer and, for the first time, Lily notices that what she took to be bath towels used to dry herself from a shower are actually a roll of bundled bedsheets held in her mother's arms. Her hair not wet from bathing, but from the sweat of recent exertion. The birth of her child.

As she watches these images, Lily's body fills with a blood-driving warmth, as if she had stopped for a couple of whisky shots at the pub outside. But in her mind, she's the opposite of drunk. Her consciousness is sharpened in anticipation of what she's about to see next.

Lily's mother spreads the sheets wider at one end to reveal a pink newborn. Eyes tightly closed, the tiny hands reaching and clenching. On the sheets the mucus and blood that show the child had arrived only moments earlier.

Michael's hand enters the frame and gently taps the baby's nose, strokes its forehead. When he tickles its hands the infant's fingers grip around his and don't let go.

"What a *strong* worm!" he says, and laughs. A real, human sound.

Who is this man? How can he be there, with the infant version of herself? But Lily is so mesmerized by what she's seeing, she can't focus on these thoughts for long. Her mother is there, right there, on the screen in front of her. As shocking as Michael's presence on the tape is, her mother's is even more miraculous.

"Stop calling her that!" her mother says, laughing herself. "Her name is Lily."

"Why Lily?"

"Because she's *pretty,* that's why."

Then it's her mother's turn to let the baby hold her finger.

It goes on like this for several seconds. A mother looking down at her newborn child, whispering her name.

Lily. Pretty little Lily.

But then a new sound comes over the TV speakers that startles the grown-up Lily so much she actually lurches back from the screen.

The man starts singing words she can't understand but that she recognizes as Hungarian. The tune she remembers her mother humming to her at bedtime when she was a child.

Lily's mother watches him. "What's that?" she asks.

"A lullaby."

"Will you teach it to me?"

"You won't understand the words."

"It's not about the words. Teach me the melody."

Michael starts to sing again, slower this time, and Lily's mother sings with him, turning the words into a sweet humming. Before she knows she's doing it, Lily is humming along to it too.

There was fear in her only a moment ago, but something more powerful has entered her, something enveloping, supple, elemental. Hidden in a London hotel room watching her parents on a recording of her first moments of life. A family divided by time, by death, now singing the same song.

Edinburgh
December 10, 1878

Another writer.

Given the decades since my meetings with Mary Shelley, this shows how well I can restrain myself. As much as I admired *Frankenstein*, Mary had gilded her fiction to such a degree that while I knew I was the creature behind the Creature, it could never be seen as a true account. What I seek now is something different. A journalist who can render my life in words—the facts instead of metaphors, reporting instead of poetry.

Over the past few months in London I

spent the days reading all the magazines where such a talent might be found. *Macmillan's*, the *Illustrated London News*. It was in one of those that I first came across Robert Louis Stevenson.

I have traveled to Edinburgh where Stevenson lives in his parents' row house on a distinguished street in New Town. Yesterday evening I walked round to the place and, when I knocked, the door was opened by a man of comical appearance. Tall, thin as a stick, his hair greasy and long, the posture of a cricket. Even his clothes were eccentric: buttoned pajamas covered by a velvet smoking jacket. Most amusing of all was his face. An oval of ever-changing expressions, the eyes bulging with mock alarm.

"Robert Stevenson?" I asked.

"If you are a bill collector, please return when my father is at home."

"I'm not here about any debt. I believe you possess something I need."

"And what is that?"

"Talent."

He giggled. A schoolboy titter that brought on a round of coughing so violent I thought he might perish right there on the doorstep.

I asked him if I might take him into town

for a drink to discuss the commission I had in mind.

He stepped out and closed the door behind him. "You may take me anywhere for a drink, good sir," he said. "But while you know my name, I have yet to learn yours."

"Michael Eszes."

"Well, Michael," the cricket said, throwing an arm across my shoulders. "I know a place where commissions are best discussed."

He directed me to a club where his attire drew attention but, after ordering oysters and two bottles of good champagne, not enough for us to be asked to leave. As we ate (or he ate, and I drank), I grew increasingly impressed by the amount of wine and then gin he put down his throat, his Adam's apple leaping up and down like the rest of him. He corrected me when I called him by his given name.

"Call me Skivvy. My friends do."

"Is that what we are now? Friends?"

"Aye. If you're paying for all this? The very best of friends." He sat back in his chair, swept his long hair behind his ears with his finger, and said he was now ready for the presentation.

"I belong to this world and the other," I told the skinny Scotsman. "I am a scholar and a monster in one man."

Skivvy looked at me with what I took to be mock seriousness.

"Careful, my friend. There's a book in that."

"It is as though I am two persons, possessed of two faces, two characters. Put together, I am hardly human at all."

"You say two faces. But I see only one."

"Come then," I said. "Let me show you the other."

We left the club with Stevenson under the impression that we were going to proceed to some other, more ribald entertainment. Instead, we lurched along George Street until I spotted a man ahead of us. I proposed we follow him. No doubt Skivvy thought it was a game. It's why he suppressed another fit of giggles and tiptoed along next to me. When we were no more than three strides behind the stranger, on a side street off Charlotte Square, our prey slowed. His head turned to us. He smiled at Stevenson. But when he took me in, he cowered.

"Oh Christ," the man said.

"No need for worry, my good—"

Stevenson began, but was interrupted when I stepped forward to spin the man around and put my boot to his knee, hard enough to rip the bone through the back of his leg. Once he was down, I kicked him again—the head this time. His skull snapped back so that he was left staring into the sky above as if counting the stars.

I turned to look at Stevenson and saw it in his face. Elongated when at rest, but now stretched farther still, the mouth agape. It wasn't only shock from witnessing an unspeakable thing, but from its opportunity.

He saw a story.

Edinburgh
December 12, 1878

Today I returned to Heriot Row and sat on one of the benches in the park directly across from the Stevensons' door. When Skivvy came out and noticed me he stopped, his face visibly gauging whether he should retreat or venture forward.

I waved at him, beckoning. He started across the street with the halting, head-swinging progress of a nervous cat.

"You can never write about me," I told him when he took a seat next to me.

"Yet you approached me for that purpose."

"I was mistaken. I was seeking objectivity, but I realize now that such a thing is impossible when it comes to storytelling."

"Well, Michael," he said, leaning away with a hand raised philosophically to his chin. "There's writing about a thing and then there's writing about a thing."

"Either one. You can't do it."

"Or you'll . . . do to me what you did to him?"

"No. I'll do it to your mother and father first. Then I'll do it to you."

He leaned even farther back as if to situate himself at the greatest distance possible from me while still remaining seated.

"I tried to tell myself you were a dream," he said. "But here you are. And I'm not asleep."

I rose, casting him in shade.

"Not a word, written or spoken," I said. "Do you understand?"

He nodded. Even as I walked off he kept his head going up and down like a pigeon's, a motion that wasn't acceptance but the labored swallowing that comes from trying not to be sick.

Writers are a strange breed. Magpies, scavengers. So fearful of the world they would prefer to describe it than live in it, yet brave to the point of idiocy when in pursuit of inspiration. The real ones will slip their heads into the noose and pull the lever themselves if they think a hanging would make a good tale.

Take Skivvy.

Last year—eight years after our first meeting—I read his *Strange Case of Dr. Jekyll and Mr. Hyde* shortly after its publication. It has caused me to pursue him over the last several months of his travels. A theft for which he will pay with his life.

I admit that the book's primary offense is against my vanity. Hyde, the monster whom the physician Jekyll becomes when he drinks a potion of his devising, is described in the most hideous terms. "Something wrong with his appearance; something displeasing, something downright detestable," Stevenson has one character say. Another struggles to provide a concrete description. "There is something more, if I could find a name for it. God bless me, the man seems hardly human! Something troglodytic, shall we say? . . ."

This was the Scotsman being vague so as not to identify me. Yet his one inexcusable offense was Hyde's most awful crime: beating a man to death in the street. This was me.

I will make him suffer for that.

Edinburgh
May 12, 1887

I came to kill Stevenson, yet as of this evening, he remains alive.

Why? I'm not sure I possess the answer. Perhaps it was sympathy. As it happened, I arrived two days before the poor man was to bury the father he loved. And then I saw him, walking alone in his mourning suit, and as I approached I must admit I could not wholly fend off pity for the chain-smoking wraith.

When he saw me he stopped, knowing it was pointless to shout, to run. I spoke to him in the simplest terms: his life might be spared, but only if he left Europe for exile in some far-off place where his chatter could not be heard. He would have to take his mother with him too, along with his wife, her daughter, and son. He would leave Scotland and London and the literary world behind or I would do things to all of them beyond his Mr. Hyde's darkest fathoming.

I do believe he will not deny me this time.

22

She was awakened by the monster knocking at the door.

Not the one at the Alaskan cabin she shared with her mother. It's the door to her room at the Montague Hotel, one she rises from the bed and goes to. Even on tiptoes the peephole is too high for her to look out of. If she wants to see what shape is on the other side she has no choice but to open the door. The same problem her mother would have faced at the cabin the day she died.

Lily opens the door.

Nothing but empty hallway. Flies buzzing around a tray of room service food left on the floor. Suddenly hungry, she squints to see what her neighbor had for dinner.

A glass of red wine too thick to be wine. Set in the center, in a nouvelle cuisine minimalist arrangement, twin pieces of oddly shaped meat, all hard ridges and curved ligament. She's about to take a step out of her room to take a closer look when she sees it's not meat at all but a set of human ears.

She jumps back inside and pushes the door shut.

"This isn't happening," she whispers.

Really? her inner voice answers. *Do you smell that?*

And now she does. Something humid and rank in the room's darkness.

That's as real as it gets.

The thought occurs to her that Michael awaits her in the bed, that the odor belongs to him.

Lily sidesteps into the bathroom and closes the door, pushing the lock button. She slides backward until she bumps against the toilet. There's a stillness long enough that she starts to believe she was mistaken about the smell but then it's back. Not coming from the bedroom but inside the bathroom where she now stands.

The shower curtain is pulled halfway shut. Did she leave it that way?

She yanks it open.

What lies in the tub is something she recognizes. The rolled bedsheet, mostly creamy and white except for an archipelago of blood at the one end. The shape of the body within it. The yellowish arms that had found their way out of the cracks. Cal's face only half covered so that his eyes, round buttons of shock, look up at her with a puppet's comical surprise.

She doesn't remember wrapping the body in a bedsheet. But Michael would have.

Lily pulls the curtain closed all the way to the tiles and turns her back on it. She studies herself in the mirror over the sink and tries to see the doctor there, the reassuring face of professional competence and sanity. In her life before this, her own image was usually enough to set her right again. Now she looks at herself and sees the face of someone on the edge of letting go.

She would stay where she is for the rest of the night but then the shower curtain moves behind her. In the mirror, she sees fingers graze the edge of the tub.

"Don't," Lily whispers.

In her mind she imagines her mother, not Cal, stepping out of the tub. Those fingers that stroked against the enamel—she sees them as familiar. Aren't those a woman's nails that now reach around the curtain's edge and start to draw it back, the metal rings screeching along the rod?

The woman's hand grips the curtain. The thing steps out of the tub and stops inches from her.

"You can look now, Lily."

Were her eyes closed? She opens them.

With relief, Lily sees that it's neither Cal nor her mother. Dr. Edmundston stands just behind her shoulder. Then she remembers that Dr. Edmundston is dead too.

"I'm so sorry, Lionel," she starts through instant tears. "I didn't know that he—"

He waves her apologies away with a hand the color of ash. "What's done is done," he says, and nearly chokes on a watery laugh. "Or should I say, what's dead is dead."

The comfort she felt at Dr. Edmundston's appearance is instantly draining away. The dead smell is growing stronger. And even though Edmundston's voice is as kindly as it was in life, there's a malignant intensity to his stare.

"Why are you here?" she asks.

"Here?" he repeats, looking around the bathroom as if for the first time. "I'm here to *help* you."

"Help me how?"

"We're psychiatrists, Lily. And I feel compelled to intervene when a colleague is—how shall I put this?—negligent in her practice."

"I don't—"

"Come now. It's all rather obvious, from a psychoanalytic point of view," he says. "Three novels, each dramatizing an antagonist bearing a unique mental deformity. The Creature: a being made of dead parts, a soul tortured by solitude. Hyde: the psychotic with dissociative identity disorder, one half the responsible physician, the other an escaped patient beyond all control. And Dracula, a projection of insatiable lust darkened by sexual anxiety. Three texts, three psychological conditions. But in this case all combined into one subject."

"You mean him. Michael."

Edmundston takes a deep breath to hide his growing impatience. "Who is Michael?"

"The man I'm following."

"Wrong."

"How do you—"

"You're following a set of symptoms. He exists only as that which you've worked to construct."

"I didn't *make* him, Lionel. He *came* to me."

"That's the thing about the human mind. All our dreams are answered one way or another."

"I didn't dream him up!" Her voice falls along with the last tethers of her certainty.

"Let me ask you something," Lionel says, raising his chin in his most doctorly pose. "Have you ever considered that the thing you seek isn't an unnatural being, isn't your long-lost father, but yourself?"

"I don't understand."

"Then let me make it clear for you, you stupid, *stupid* girl."

Edmundston changes. The hatred—Lily sees now that that's what it is—twists his features, his body stiffening as it floods through him. His calm physician's voice replaced by a snarling threat as his skin dries and sucks against the bone.

"The one you call Michael isn't a living thing. He's a fucking diagnosis," he hisses before gripping his cold hands around her throat. "The *real* monster, my dear, is you."

23

Lily lies on the bathroom's tiled floor. The door is open. It's the first thing she sees when she opens her eyes.

The second thing is a Lyceum Theatre playbill for *The Lion King* that had been placed on her chest.

She doesn't remember anything after the imagined Lionel—the rather more-than-imagined Lionel—set to choking the life out of her. Who made him go away and opened the door if it wasn't her?

You know who. The same one who left the playbill behind. Another come hither. Know what you shouldn't *do? Take the bait. Take a pill instead. On second thought? Take two.*

She does.

It allows her to look into the tub to confirm that no body lies there and then stand under the shower's hot water long enough that she comes out pink and steaming. After getting dressed, she leaves the hotel. Once she's out on Bloomsbury's elegant, brick-faced streets, she can think more clearly.

At the first bank she comes to she ducks inside and withdraws as much cash as she can from her checking account. No more plastic from now on. She figures it's at least one of the ways Will, Black Parka, and whoever else have been tracking her. It leaves her feeling lighter, almost ghostly.

After buying a bacon sandwich she eats as she goes, she consults a map and decides on a route that will take her to the Lyceum Theatre. She walks the whole way. For some reason she feels sure that no one is following her at the moment. It's not only the casting off of credit cards that does it, but the sharpening of her intuition.

The Lyceum is one of the grander West End houses, with a wide façade of white plaster columns and towering signage. She doesn't expect any of the doors to be unlocked but tries them anyway. The third one opens. It's the box office mezzanine, which would explain the open door. Yet all the wickets are closed, the place quieter than it ought to be.

Lily crosses the carpeted lobby and steps into the auditorium's Orchestra seating. The stage set is in some midpoint of rearrangement: a cliffside here, a grass field there, a hot African sun on a background screen. Yet no stagehands push any of it about, no techies in black T-shirts talking into headsets. That's when she realizes it's Monday. The only day of the week most of London's theaters are dark.

"Over here."

When she squints, his shadowed form can be seen sitting alone in the second-to-last row.

"Come," Michael says.

Lily slides in from the aisle and takes the seat two over from him, leaving him slightly out of reach.

"I watched the video," she says. "You weren't lying. You really did know my mother. And me."

"But you've known that all along, haven't you?"

"A part of me did, I think. But it wasn't until I heard you sing—"

"That you knew for certain I am your father."

"Yes." Lily nods, and keeps nodding as the cool lines of tears wet her lips.

He looks toward the stage, casts his eyes over the yellows and oranges of African savannah, but sees something else.

"Have you ever heard of Henry Irving?" he asks, and Lily is too puzzled by the question to ask one of her own.

"Was he a friend of Robert Louis Stevenson's?"

"No, no. Not a writer! After Skivvy I wanted nothing more to do with that untrustworthy breed. Yet I still yearned for something more than the existence of a predator. I had sampled

213

all manner of drink and drugs, but perhaps being immortal muted their danger. Sex provided momentary distraction, but for whatever reason my seed is incompatible with the human egg, so that all my couplings were only that. What remained?"

"The theater?"

Michael nods at her guess and Lily looks up at the stage. "Irving was an actor. This was where he worked," he says. "I saw every play and cheap spectacle that London had to offer, from Shakespeare to silly illusionists, opera to pantomime. The only productions I avoided were those of *Jekyll and Hyde*, which plagued the West End at the time. But Irving's shows were distinct. Flamboyant, sentimental. Enormous undertakings that required a great number of 'supers,' or extras, each paid two shillings a night. It was work that allowed one to share the stage with the great man, to look out at the audience through the haze of gas footlights and see the hundreds of faces stricken in amazement or sobbing with emotion. At least, that's what I saw when I was among a hundred and fifty others who trooped across the boards as a fully manned army in *The Lady of Lyons*."

Michael turns to Lily and though she tries to keep her eyes on the stage, she can't help but face him.

"Irving was the primary owner of the Lyceum

as well as its star, but the day-to-day managing of the place was left to a broad bear of an Irishman," he says. "His name was Bram Stoker. And for the better part of the year 1890, he was my friend."

Lily hears the creak of his seat and knows that Michael has bent closer to her.

"It was Stoker who hired me," he says, his voice a tremor through the metal frame she sits on, moving through her. "When I sat before his desk wild with papers and open bottles of ink, he asked where I was from, and when I said Hungary he called it the last place where people still believed in fairies. I replied that I would have thought Ireland would still be a candidate for belief in such nonsense, and just when I thought I'd said too much, he roared with laughter. 'Quite so, Mr. Eszes!' he bellowed. 'Though our Irish fairies lack the menace of your gypsy versions!' "

"Menacing fairies. A gypsy," Lily says. "He saw you as research."

"A possibility I failed to consider when he invited me to the Beefsteak Room, the club located upstairs here. Of course you are thinking I should have known better. And you would be right. That initial interest in gypsies and Eastern European folktales was a signal of writerly strategies. But over our first dinner Stoker was so affable, so full of backstage gossip, I took him as the contented company manager he appeared to be. In fact I thought I recognized in him what

I had discovered in myself: the satisfaction of being around artists that came free of longing to be one. It was far from the only night Bram and I stayed up late in the Beefsteak Room. And it was far from the only room we stayed up late in."

Michael rises and takes the seat directly next to Lily. He doesn't touch her, but she can feel him now just the same. The outline of him, the shadowed creases of his features like a sheet enfolding her in darkness.

"I should explain, Lily, an aspect to my powers I have so far neglected to share," he says. "If I choose, I can feed on the blood of a human while at the same time forcing some of my own blood into them. The result, when successful, is an individual who is neither dead nor alive, enslaved to my command. They don't last long. I cannot make them live on like me as the Count does in *Dracula*. But it was Stoker's experience with three such creatures that was the genesis for his novel."

The auditorium dims as if someone is at the lighting board, quieting the audience before the first notes of the prelude. But Lily tells herself it's only her consciousness dancing along the edge of night, pulling itself back from fainting.

"I had made arrangements to entrap three young women in a rented room off Oxford Street," he says, and Lily hangs on to his words. "Call my luck good or bad, but each of them had taken to the process. They had lost their color, but none of their beauty, and only part of their lives. Have you read Stoker's pig slop of a novel, Lily? The protagonist, Harker, is trapped inside the Count's castle when three female vampires try to seduce him. Before the moment of consummation, Dracula intervenes, declaring, 'This man belongs to me!' When did Stoker jot this episode in his notes? Two days later I opened the door to that room off Oxford Street and the creatures I made rose from their blankets, eyeing the big Irishman with a hunger that could easily be mistaken for lust. Unlike Harker, Stoker showed little hesitation in submitting to the young women's attentions. I will spare you the details, my daughter, but I'm sure you can imagine the whole writhing scene. For Stoker's sake, it was a good thing I lingered. One, and then another, and then all three girls' expressions changed from false arousal to real craving, their teeth closing in on Bram's throat. 'Stop!' I shouted. 'This man is not yours! He belongs to me!' "

Lily starts to shake. Not a passing shiver at the projection of this scene on the darkened stage before her, but a series of uncontrolled jolts that brings an echoing squeak from the seat under her. Michael's hand lands on top of hers and her body stills, even if the shrieking of her mind grows even louder.

"We repaired to a public house," he says. "And

what I did next may puzzle you, Lily, given my declaration of never revealing myself to a writer ever again. But Bram Stoker *wasn't* a writer. And in any case, I didn't tell him everything. The tale I spun had nothing to do with Dr. Eszes, or the innumerable deaths required to keep me alive. Instead I spoke of myself as a kind of magician, a hypnotist who could put spells on people like the young women in the Soho room. Stoker nodded at all this. For a time our conversation turned to other things, the lewd jokes that used to delight us, but it was different now. It's why I was surprised, a couple days on, when he asked me to the Beefsteak Room again. He came right to the point, asking if the people of my country still believed in vampires. I played along. Told him that there had been for many centuries in that part of the world tales of human-appearing parasites that existed on the blood of the living, but they were no more special—and no more real—than the forest witch who breastfeeds the trees. Stoker leaned forward. 'You've told me you are a magician. Yet that's not really what you are, is it, Michael?' He knew. He knew, and I saw myself killing him, saw the spray of his blood on the wallpaper. It took all my will to excuse myself. I left London the next morning."

Lily tries to stand, even to lean away from him, but she can do nothing more than what the deeper part of her wants to do.

"But you came back," she manages to say.

"To the same seat you're sitting in now. It was several years after our last dinner in the Beefsteak Room that I walked past the Lyceum doors and saw '*Dracula*, a Play by Bram Stoker' on a poster out front. You must understand that in those days the public reading of a play was not done for the purpose of rehearsing, but to assert copyright over a forthcoming text. It's why I read that poster and knew at once that *Dracula* was to be a book."

Michael takes an abrupt gulp of breath, followed by a kind of growl, and Lily recognizes it as an involuntary utterance of contempt. Along with a rage that doesn't wholly belong to Michael, but to his demonic other half.

"The date was set for the following morning. Wearing a hat, scarf, and spectacles to obscure my face, I went," he goes on. "Bram stood behind a lectern at one corner of the stage, reading the play aloud. It was awful. Irving himself slipped in and stood in the aisle before declaring *Dreadful!* and walking out. I too left before the end. Outside, I stood among the throng going this way and that along the Strand and told myself there was little harm that could come out of a book taken from the text of such a lifeless play. I was proven wrong. *Dracula*'s success pained me so much more than Mary's or Skivvy's. To see how Stoker's bogus exaggerations—wooden stakes! crosses! coffins for beds!—became embedded in the world's imagination was too much to bear. I was humiliated. Jealous too. At least the Count was known to the world, however ridiculous. I remained in oblivion. And then, at some point after the two world wars, I started to feel hunted, as if the twentieth century itself wished to see me brought to ground."

He wipes the back of his hand over his lips but remains silent. It occurs to Lily that this turn in his story may be a buried hint that he knows about Will.

"Yet there was something unexpected, possibly enchanted, that occurred over this second half of my life," he says, his voice dwindling to a whisper. "There was you."

She feels again that something physical is about to happen between them, an embrace or the infliction of pain, something shocking. But the moment is interrupted by the sound of sirens outside the theater's walls. It brings Michael to his feet.

As he squeezes past her knees he takes her by the hand, pulling her up, so that she follows him down the aisle to the orchestra pit and around to a door that takes them backstage. Lily keeps pace at something between her fastest walk and a run. Either he knows the way in the darkness of the stage's wings, or his vision is that of a nocturnal bird of prey, because though Lily catches sight of hanging ropes and sandbags and soundboards they don't slam into any of it.

She's blinded by the gray London light that hits her when he crashes through the stage door. Unlike their previous partings when he's slipped away once he's determined they haven't been observed, this time he doesn't let go of her hand.

"Stay close," he says, before pulling her down the narrow lane and into the noise of the Strand.

24

They don't go far before Michael takes an abrupt turn off the curb and pulls Lily into oncoming traffic.

She squeezes her eyes shut, readying herself for the impact. All around her are blaring horns, the swirled air of cabs and double deckers passing within inches. But nothing hits her. When she opens her eyes they've slowed to a walk under the silver awning of the Savoy Hotel where a doorman sweeps his top hat inches from the ground in a bow.

Michael slips a hundred-pound note into his hands. "You haven't seen us," he says.

They enter the marble lobby and proceed directly to the elevators. Lily wonders how they would appear to others in this place. A man you would describe as foreign, totally assured in his movements. A woman following after him as if he's all she has. They would appear as lovers, certainly. Caught up in their own world, dashing into an elevator and the man pressing his floor with the urgency of anticipated pleasure.

They get out and go to the end of the hallway where Michael keys open a door that leads into a narrow entranceway before expanding into a grand suite. A king-size bed under an oil painting of the Houses of Parliament, the real thing visible through the broad wall of windows that overlooks the Thames. In the middle of the room there's a round mahogany dining table with an ice bucket on a silver tray, a bottle of Pol Roger poking its head out the top.

"I hope you like champagne," he says, already striding to the table where he pulls out the cork with a muted pop and expertly pours them full flutes of amber bubbles. Lily considers making a run for the door, but then she remembers she came to London looking for him. For better or worse, foolishness or necessity. And now she's here. Running now would be like running from herself.

"This was Churchill's favorite, you know," Michael says, passing a glass to her. "It's said he had a bottle to himself every day at lunch."

"Easy for him. What did he have to do in the afternoons? Save the free world?"

Michael laughs, and it starts her laughing. She

hasn't yet taken a sip and she feels intoxicated, the plush gilt and varnished wood surfaces of the room pitching slightly, as if the whole of London had just pushed away from a pier.

"To you, Lily," he says, and clinks her glass. "My brave girl who has come all the way to the end."

They drink. The wine so cold and sweet it doesn't seem possible that it was composed of natural elements alone.

"This is an unusual indulgence for me, but I believe the occasion calls for it," he says, breaking his lock on her eyes and looking around at the room's ornate finishes. He motions for her to sit in one of the two chairs at the table and Lily is happy to take her place there, not trusting her legs to hold her up any longer without swaying. "In America, I favor the roadside motels, the mom-and-pop places with their rust-stained pools. Europe and Asia are easier. Every fourth door is a guesthouse with a handwritten registry and a manager happy to ignore missing sheets for a price. All paid with paper that leaves no trace behind."

"I've adopted the same practice myself," Lily says, taking another sip.

She sees his hand tighten around his glass so that she's sure it will shatter in his fist.

"You have seen them again," he says.

"Yes."

"Have you spoken with them?"

"No."

He studies her long enough with his dead eyes that she's about to scream. Before she does, his face relaxes again, the hold on the glass loosens, and he drinks what remains in it.

"Who are they?" she asks.

"I'm not precisely sure. It's not any regular police force—they're too clever, and move too freely between nations for that. Their numbers are renewed, year after year, so that just when I can recognize one of their agents a new one comes along to take me by surprise."

Lily wants to ask about her mother, the video, the completion of the circle that connects them, but recognizes she'll have to come at these things indirectly, waiting for an opening he won't back away from when she takes advantage of it.

"Let's assume they want to destroy you to prevent you from destroying others," she says. "You can understand their objective, can't you?"

"I have gone from being born of history, to being part of it, to standing outside it altogether. A virus immune to the human events you think of as momentous," he says, moving to the window and following the passage of a glass-ceilinged tourist boat below. "The destruction of others? Nothing can alter the course that mankind has chosen for itself. Not war or famine or the election of saviors. Your march toward the end will continue, unslowed. There will be drought and starvation and the extinction of species, one by one. In the final hours, there will only be the last of the survivors. The fiercest, most unhesitant killer. There will only be me."

He continues to look out at the river below where another round of wailing sirens suggests a recent car accident or medical emergency taking place on the embankment. Lily's curiosity is not enough to lend her the strength to get up to see which.

"So long as you see yourself existing outside history, you can cause as much pain as you like. Is that it?"

"What is the appropriate price to maintain an existence of true singularity?" he says, turning from the window, his face a featureless silhouette against the gray English sky. "Over my time I have killed tens of thousands, most for sustenance, though admittedly a good number— five thousand? six?—for pleasure alone. Yet I have witnessed civil wars, already fading from memory, that have put more bodies in the ground. Am I not worth a Balkan conflict, a Somalia, a Pinochet here and there?"

Lily opens her mouth to speak but he raises his hand to silence her.

"I merely propose a calculation," he continues, stepping close to place his hands on the table. "The same thing generals and kings have done for millennia, and what presidents and CEOs do today: an accounting of lives in the achievement of some greater goal. Collateral damage. Isn't this the term?"

"How can one life be worth the lives of thousands?"

"It's not in *me* that my value lies, but in the ideas that attach themselves to me. I am not a prophet. I am a monster."

He moves to her side and pours himself another glass of champagne, watches the bubbles rise with the attention of a scholar reading the scroll of some ancient history. She reaches for her glass but doesn't trust that her hand is up to the job, and ends up leaving her arm upturned on the table as if awaiting a needle.

There is so much she needs to ask him but the questions slip free every time she thinks she's captured one. She takes a moment to find her balance and ends up considering his face and, for the first time, sees herself in him. His mouth, his finest feature, the same shape as her own. Or is this, the psychiatrist in her wonders, only a narcissistic distortion? Rendering her desire acceptable by seeing it as an admiration of herself.

"What is it to be you?" she asks finally.

"You are being the doctor again."

"I'm being curious."

"Well then. Pretend we are sitting together

outside, the two of us," he says, and Lily is instantly alive to the sensation of it: his body next to hers, the coolness of the air, a broad square before them. It comes to her that this isn't a scene she's imagining. It's a scene he's putting in her mind. "A child walking, holding his father's hand. I watch them and wonder what it would be like to hold that hand, to love and care so simply, just as I also wonder what the boy's blood would taste like, the pitch of the father's screams. I can feel these things—the impulse to kill, the tender yearnings of a parent—without contradiction."

He turns from her and the motion breaks the connection, leaves her mind unoccupied of the horror she'd just pictured. Now when he speaks he moves about the room, touching the bedcover, surveying the art on the wall.

"You would think someone who has seen so many hideous acts—who has delivered them with his own hands—would be immune to beauty, but the opposite is true," he says. "Every day offers the unexpected, even as I lay out traps like Prufrock's coffee spoons, city to city, death to death. It can be a drudgery, all the space between killing. But then something wondrous appears: the way the sun emerges from behind the clouds and lightens a century's worth of soot from a wall of brick, a man carrying flowers to his lover's apartment. So many versions of the same sights and sounds—but I am still moved! For a moment. Inevitably, the sun sets again and the hunger returns and I remember my grim place in the course of things."

"Which is what?"

"To embody the fears of two centuries' worth of collective imaginings, a thing every mother promises cannot be real. The Bard's Danish prince debated between being and not being. My fate is to know I am forever both."

"What about my mother?" Lily says, arriving at the question she'd wanted to ask, now seizing an opportunity to voice it for the first time. "Did you love her?"

"I tried to. Wanted to."

"Did you—" she starts, and the room spins again. "Do you love me?"

He steps away to sit on the edge of the bed and part of her wants to go to him. Lily can't tell if this would be to hold him, or kiss him, or simply stand over him to see what it's like to have him look up at her.

His mouth opens. What comes out is a song.

The same lullaby Lily remembers her mother singing to her, the one Michael voiced in the video. The melody all the more haunting for being sung in a language she can't understand.

"What do the words mean?" Lily says when he's finished.

" 'May you grow to be strong. May the night be

free of bad dreams. May I watch you become a woman.' A rough paraphrase."

Lily wipes her eyes, expecting her hand to come away wet from tears, but finds the skin dry. "You haven't answered my question," she says.

"You were an infant, easy to be proud of but impossible to know. Love? I mostly responded to the instinct of protection. No one would do you harm, not so long as I lived."

"I meant now."

He closes his eyes as if thinking of the best way to deliver what she's asked for at the same time as he places his hands on his knees. They're the kind of hands she likes. Strong and roughened by work. And then she remembers the kind of work that has left its mark on him and looks away.

"You are aware of my past attempts to transform a mortal into a being like myself," he says. "I stopped trying for many years after the girls I'd half-turned for Stoker in that Soho room. And then I met the woman who would become your mother."

Lily's training tells her she must try to appear indifferent to whatever spell he's cast on the air of the room, pulling her deeper into him with each breath.

But you can stop fighting now, her inner voice counters. *Let go. Be part of it. Part of him.*

"Who was she?"

"Even as a girl Alison was considered to be

229

possessed of dark gifts," he says. "This was in the Florida Panhandle in the early 1960s. People would come to the house where she grew up and, for a fee her parents would collect, she would tell them pieces of the future, or converse with the dead, or lay her hands on them to relieve their pain. They called her what her grandmother had been called two generations earlier."

"A healer?"

"A witch."

"Was she?"

"Depends on what one means by the term," he says. "Her nanna had certainly acquainted her with the making of tonics, passed down a book of cures that involved incantations. All just primitive snake oil for the most part. But she went further with it than her grandmother ever did. She always told me it was like she was being guided by a dark hand, one that showed her how to bring natural things together in a way that brought about unnatural results."

"How far did she go?"

"So far it frightened her. Once she was older she wanted only to be free of that place. But the dark hand was always with her."

"It made her run away."

"Only to find there was nowhere to run. She was a wanderer, just like me. A shared burden that drew us together. The demon in me and the magic in her. But when I entered the tent at a traveling carnival outside Huntsville, Texas, to have my fortune told, I knew she would be the one even before she took hold of my hand. 'I see a change,' she told me. 'I see a light, and blood, and life. I see a girl.' It was her own future she was reading as much as mine."

Lily moves the arm she's reminded still lies atop the table and knocks her glass over, the champagne making a river on the reflective wood and dripping off the side. Neither of them move to right it.

"You decided to try with her," she says.

"Yes."

"And it worked? You turned her into whatever you are?"

"Enough for us to conceive a child. Enough for her to be stronger, age more slowly than others. She was half human and half me. We both feared that attempting to push her all the way would be too much. And soon there was a baby to consider. There was a change, just as she foresaw."

"Did she . . . hunt?"

"Some of the time. She was halfway in that respect too. I had teeth and claws like mine made for her, and I tried to teach her how to use them. But as much as she longed for blood—as much as she needed it—she was hesitant. I often had to do the work for her."

A picture of her mother comes to Lily. One with the steel teeth in her mouth, her face smeared with blood. The horror in her eyes as she swallowed.

"What about after I was born?" Lily asks. "Did she still feed that way?"

"Never again. She was resolved to be as human as she could for your sake."

"How long did you stay with her?"

"I didn't leave her side the first year. But it was increasingly difficult to hide the three of us from the hunters and the police. We parted, but not before we had devised a system of sending letters to post office boxes, an improvised code of meeting places so that I could see the two of you. But even this proved dangerous. It was essential that the hunters not know you existed. And so your mother kept moving, I kept moving. Until we decided on the cabin."

"A home."

"A place as far away from the world as the world permits."

"But they still found us."

"They found *her.*"

"I don't understand."

He rises from the edge of the bed and he appears a foot taller than before, wider too. Swelling and lengthening as he floats closer.

"She thought the hunters could keep her safer than I could. She had regrets over what she had become, what she blamed me for. So she left a note for them, told them where I was. They ambushed me and I knew she was the cause. Even the hunters confirmed it. 'Your lady friend sold you out,' one of them said, though they were the last words he ever spoke."

"What did you do?"

"I came to the cabin. And there, something strange occurred. Something that has never happened to me before or since."

He spreads his arms out from his sides, so wide Lily thinks he'll be able to touch the window with one and the far wall with the other.

"I was the horse you rode on, Lily," he says, and his eyes seem to round to resemble those of the animal he describes. "A white Lipizzaner like the ones old Eszes kept. I couldn't have gotten you out of there before you either froze to death or the hunters came to take us both down. So I asked God to change me—I *prayed,* Lily! Though I don't believe it was Him who did it. Something so strong it reshaped me, as the poets say only love has the power to do."

He stops when he's a half step away from her, brings in one of his arms, and runs a finger through the puddle of champagne on the table.

Stay away.

She sees it now. This was the lesson her mother wished to impart to her daughter, a lesson Lily was too young to discern at the time. Lily's mother—Alison—worried she might one day meet this man, and he would share the same stories of his remarkable origins as he had shared with her. Dracula, Mr. Hyde, Victor Frankenstein's creature. The bedtime horror stories her mother told were a warning, not against talking to strangers or getting lost in the woods, but against Michael.

And now a whisper of her mother's voice is summoned to Lily's mind. Not anything she said in life but something she calls out to her daughter now from the other side.

Run.

The intent of the stories she told, the gun lessons and survival tips and the instilled instinct to find a secret place, of everything her mother did to prepare Lily if she ever had to face her father.

Run like I should have run.

But Lily hadn't run anywhere except to him. She'd listened to his stories and come to believe them, fallen for them, been fascinated by them just as her mother had. And like her, she'd allowed herself to wonder what it would be like to be a part of them, someone who plays a crucial part in an extraordinary history-in-progress, a late-arriving character who sets the plot on a new course.

She was frightened by the stories her mother told when she was five and six years old, just as she was frightened by Michael's telling of his monstrous past, but in both cases not frightened enough. There is revulsion in our response to what we fear, but as the psychiatrist in Lily knows, there can be, for some, an attraction too.

"Was it you, Michael?" she asks, her voice breaking, falling away. "Did you kill her?"

"Listen to me—"

"You *did,* didn't you?"

"Lily—"

"You fucking bastard! You *did!* You lying—"

He grabs her wrist and it instantly silences her.

"The hunters were coming. Maybe a day behind me, maybe only hours," he says. "They would destroy your mother and me both. But they didn't know about you. You were the one who could still be saved."

He releases her, and her anger, at least the frothing surface of it, is released as swiftly as it appeared. There's only the weight of acceptance, the already-dwindling, childish resistance to fact.

"But why did she have to die?"

He bends low, using his wet finger to draw a square on the table with streaks of champagne. And then, within it, smaller squares in rows. A chessboard.

"Look ahead to the way the pieces would have moved," he says, now drawing lines through the squares, engagements and traps. "They wouldn't have left her alone after their failed attempt on my life. They would have tried to use her to lure me again, and if that didn't work, they would have gotten rid of her. And in doing so, they would have discovered you."

When he's finished speaking he wipes the table clean with his palm.

"You had to make it look as though the line ended with her," Lily says, finishing his reasoning for him.

"That's right."

"Did they know you'd attempted to turn others before?"

"Yes. And they knew Alison was the only one I'd had any success with."

"Which meant they would pursue you alone if they saw that she was dead. They wouldn't be looking for me."

"You would be safe. To grow up, to become what you are."

Lily smells his breath and is surprised by its sweetness. Instead of the animal odors she'd detected before, she finds herself suddenly hungry, as if the last thing he'd eaten was freshly baked bread.

"How much of my mother's blood is mine? What does it make me?"

"Only you can answer that." He pauses, taking her in with his gray eyes. "Because you believe me, don't you?"

"I do," she says, and it echoes in her head with the solemnity of a marriage vow.

He lifts her hand and guides her to the bed.

There is some vague speculating over what he might do to her, but she's not really concentrating on that yet, as if it's a troublesome errand she has to run tomorrow but hasn't the time to worry about today.

"There's something you've wished for from me, isn't there?" she says as they take their steps over the lush carpet. "Me coming after you, the journal—it hasn't only been about showing me who I am. You want me to join you."

"I will do only what you ask me to," he says when they reach the bed and she sits.

"And after? What do we do then? Run from the hunters together? Kill together?"

He sits next to her. "We can live forever," he whispers. It feels to Lily like she's lying against the ground and finding for the first time that she can hear the earth speak. "A father and daughter walking together to witness the end of time."

She has never felt anything like she does right now, at once revolted and comforted, wanting to run for the door while wanting to turn his head to her and trace the outline of his lips.

Lily looks down and sees his hand is at the top of her chest, just below her collarbone, pressing her down, a gentle weight easing her back onto the bed.

"In the morning, you will go to Hampstead Heath," he says. "I will meet you there."

Her eyes are closed. She feels as though she's

being swallowed into the softness under her, down and down, buried alive but able to breathe through the soil. It would be a nightmare if it wasn't so real, so thrilling. She is part of life and part of death, some elements growing and others receding, all of her prickling with the awareness of one thing turning into another.

25

L ily opens her eyes to a cluster of stars directly above her, so close she feels that if she raised her arms she could touch them.

She remembers Michael but not the things he said. She recalls his touch and feels a belated shriek halfway up her throat.

It's by force of will that she doesn't let it out. His words coming to her now, the information that fights to be considered first. She's also able to see that it isn't stars above her, but a crystal chandelier in the darkness.

He told you he's a monster and you believe him. So who's the psycho now?

"Both of us," she answers herself.

But you don't think that. You think you two are the only ones in the world who know the truth.

"Yes," she says, and hears herself laugh. An alien sound that instead of comforting her makes her realize she's in even worse shape than she thought.

He's where today's vampires and homicidal split personalities and the walking dead all come from.

"Yes."

Okay. Definitely both of you then.

Once she's sitting straight up on the bed she can look out the window at the black river, the yellow dome of electric light over south London held tight by low clouds. She sees herself reflected in the window, a ghost face hovering in a room decorated with antiques. It could be a hundred years ago. It could be two hundred years.

It takes cold water splashed on her face and two of her pills for Lily to shake free of him and let the rage fill the space he leaves behind. She had been half hypnotized by him for the time he circled about her in the room, enchanted by a cocktail of surprise and champagne and fear.

But that was gone now.

He killed her mother so he could go on killing. Her mother, who fought so hard against illness and poverty all for her baby, to keep her safe, keep her from him. He's murdered thousands in the name of giving life to nightmares. And now he wants Lily to join him. For her to kill too.

Michael was the monster who knocked at the cabin door.

She dresses, her clothes smelling of the horse stable scent of his skin. An exciting musk in his presence, but in his absence merely the sourness of urine and straw.

To stop herself from drifting around the room she turns on the TV. The news. An anchorwoman reporting on a breaking item about a "grim discovery in the River Thames." And then a photo of the victim, one she recognizes. The boy whose image she'd seen on the TV screens in the shop window on Oxford Street. The twelve-year-old with big ears wearing a Spurs jersey.

Lily listens to the details and knows it was Michael who did this even as the evidence aligns in her mind. The body strangely drained of blood as in a stabbing though without apparent wounds consistent with a knife attack. Then the screen shows the place where the remains were found. The north side of the river at the rear of the Savoy. The police lights and sirens that had prompted their exit of the Lyceum and, later, that Michael had looked out upon from the suite's window, without reaction, as he spoke to her about being the last of the survivors.

He'd taken the boy. Fed on his blood. And when he was done he'd thrown what was left into the cold gray of the Thames.

Lily turns off the TV. Goes to the phone and presses the number that Will gave her and that she memorized before tearing up his card.

Revenge, her inner voice tells her. *For the boy in the river. Your mother. For you.*

Lily is going to make him pay for what she saw him do when she was six years old. The Spurs jersey boy too. All of them. She's going to do it because he's the reason she can only see the world as the place where monsters hide. She's dedicated her life to naming their sicknesses and helping put them away but in the end they just keep coming.

"Lily?"

She hears Will's voice and presses the earpiece against her as if bringing him closer.

"He told me everything. What he is." *What I am,* she almost adds, but stops herself.

"What is he?"

He's my father. "He kills people for their blood."

"We know that."

"He's been alive for over two hundred years."

"We know that too."

"He wants me to be with him."

"Be with him? How?"

"By turning me into whatever he is."

There's no going back now. She has betrayed Michael just as her mother did, though for different reasons. Her mother did it for her, and Lily is doing it for her mother. For every mother who has lost a child to the bogeyman.

"Where are you now?" Will asks.

"The Savoy."

"Is he still with you?"

"No."

"Did he say where he was going?"

"No. But I think I can bring him to me."

"Okay," he says. "We need to talk. But not on the phone. Not with you in that room."

"Where do I go?"

"The lobby. Get out now. I'll be there in fifteen minutes."

26

The entrance of the Savoy at night is different from the place Lily swept through during the day. It's that Michael was holding her hand, which turned everything around her into a blur. She sits in one of the leather chairs and watches the strains of global super-wealth parade before her in their black ties and gowns and burkas and turbans.

When she sees Will enter she stands, but he walks right by without looking her way. She nearly calls his name before she gets it: he's intentionally not looking at her.

Will glances at his watch, then heads for the doors. Lily counts to five and follows him out to the drive in front of the hotel where there's a BMW 7 Series sedan with black tinted windows that he gets into. She slips in the back and the car starts off before she's closed the door.

"I like your new hair," Will says.

He's sitting next to her, but it's so dark he's little more than a presence, his leather jacket the same tar color as the interior. Even his face is smoothed by shadow.

"Where are we going?" she asks.

"Nowhere. It's safer when we're moving."

"Safer from him?"

"Yes. But there's other considerations too."

"Like?"

"Surveillance cameras. Witnesses. We're the good guys, but we're still doing something several miles outside the law."

The possibility that this all might end with her going to prison hadn't occurred to Lily. She is helping total strangers kidnap someone in a city far from home. People don't get away with that sort of thing, do they? And yet she trusts this man to get her out before it will come to that.

"He asked to meet me in the morning," she says.

"Where?"

"Hampstead Heath."

He smiles, though it looks like a grimace. Lily tells herself he's likely trained to be sweet to people in her position, make them feel like they're friends. His scars could be something he uses to his advantage, the disarming reactions of pity mistaking disfigurement for harmlessness. It doesn't matter. She likes him. She appreciates the way he wears his hurt on the outside.

"You mentioned on the phone that he wants the two of you to be together," he says. "What do you mean by that, exactly?"

"Exactly? I don't know. But he can get into my head. When my thoughts are loud, he can read me."

It feels safe floating through the night streets alone with this man. The notion of anonymous handlers back in Washington aware of their every move makes her want to propose running away with him, right now, disappearing with the only living human being she knows this side of the ocean.

"In the morning, you go to Hampstead Heath just like he told you," Will is saying. "We'll be there too."

"You mean to arrest him? I'm not sure that'll be so easy."

"We'll sedate him first. We have tranq darts that would probably kill a fit hundred-and-ninety-pound man, but should disable him until we can vacate the scene."

"Where will you take him after that?"

"That's above my pay grade."

"But you'll take his blood? Save lives?"

"That's the idea."

He's done things like this before, perhaps a

number of times. He's stolen other men in other places. But he's got something else in this game and she can see it even in the back of a dark car at night.

"Why is this so important to you?"

"It's my job. I'm good at it," he says. "And this guy, he's like no other target I've encountered. He has extraordinary talents. And he's very, very bad."

There's an opaque plastic divider between the backseat and where the driver sits. Lily looks for one, but doesn't see any sliding window she could open to look up front.

"What about you?" she asks. "Has Michael seen you?"

"No. I'll stay close the whole way so I can be there when he shows up."

"He'll know it's a trap."

"He's the one who set the time of day and place, not us. He trusts you, right?"

"Yes."

Lily remembers the way Michael's expression had changed when he spoke of her mother's betrayal. The glimpse of the thing inside him that is pure rage. Mr. Hyde. She doesn't ever want to see him look at her that way.

The car comes to a stop and Lily's hand is on the handle when Will reaches over to grip her by the arm. He means it as a transfer of strength from him to her, and in the moment they're together, it works. When he lets her go her blood rushes to her fingers, tingling as if from a thousand tiny bites.

"See you on the other side," he says before she closes the door. She wants to open it again to tell him something more, tell him everything, but the car is already pulling away and taking the corner, sleek as a shark.

27

It's just after seven the next morning when she leaves the Savoy. The moment she's outside London hits her with bus exhaust and the rattling of taxi engines. She can't stop from checking her peripheral vision to see if Will is waiting for her somewhere, perhaps holding an opened newspaper or pretending to window-shop the way spies do in movies, but she can find no one doing either of these things. She worries that she's too early, that Will and whoever else is supposed to have her back have lost her already. Even if they're so good at this sort of thing that she's being trailed without her seeing it, could the hunters be any better at it than Michael?

Lily reminds herself that he's not here on the Strand but somewhere on Hampstead Heath waiting for her. She makes her way through the crowds heading to work, repeating a single phrase—*He trusts you*—until it gains the weight of certainty in her head.

When the street opens up onto Trafalgar Square she consults her tourist map to find the location of the Charing Cross entrance to the tube. As she takes the stairs down, the city's smells are replaced with a combination of disinfectant and machine oil. It makes her stomach lurch.

While there's a stop for Hampstead Heath it would require a transfer and to keep things simple she decides to get onto the Northern line to Belsize Park instead. It will mean a longer walk from the station but she would prefer to be out in the light, plainly visible, than end up entering the heath alone.

As she waits on the jammed platform she squeezes her back against the curving wall and again tries to spot Will or one of his agents. They would be big, wouldn't they? The sort of men or women with combat expertise, muscled and wide. Yet all Lily can see are English commuters, round-shouldered and hair still wet from their showers, yawning and gazing at their phones.

Something's wrong.

It comes all at once. The sense of misalignment in the details around her, the bluish fluorescent tubes in the ceiling, the false-sounding bits of overheard conversation. All of it presenting itself to her as the unseen things that dogs bark at.

For someone so smart, you can be so fucking stupid.

This time, both Lily and the voice inside her are in complete agreement.

She was wrong to put her life into the hands of Will, a man she doesn't know. At least she's confident about what Michael is. The ones who hunt him are, if anything, more of a mystery than a two-hundred-year-old man.

The train creates a damp wind preceding its appearance from out of the tunnel's mouth. As it slows, the people around her inch closer to the doors, squeezing Lily along with them.

She holds back as much as possible so that once she's on the train she's close to the doors. Maybe she can slip out before her stop. Maybe she can run up to the street above, hail a taxi, and escape all this, let Michael and Will play out their game without her. It's not her business. What's happening now, the panicked knocking of her heart, the complicity in an operation no police or government is officially aware of—there's no need for her to be part of any of it. She's a woman who can keep a secret. She and Mary Shelley have this in common.

Lily is ready to slip through the doors when the lights go out.

Her fellow passengers have seen this before, judging from their sighs and muttered *Bloody hell*s. Even when the train shudders to a stop in the tunnel midway between Tottenham Court Road and Goodge Street there's only the slightest evidence of alarm from those around her. The gasp of a claustrophobe an arm's length away from Lily, a woman who now looks straight above her as if struggling to find the air above the water's surface. The single, alarmed shout of *No!* from a male voice at the far end of the car.

I told you something's wrong, Lily's voice says.

A minute passes.

The claustrophobic woman drops her head to look directly at Lily. Through the near-darkness her panic contorts her face and holds it that way, so that she could be wearing a personalized mask of horror.

Another minute.

There was a rumbling of the train's engine underfoot that promised they could start moving again at any moment that now goes silent. The lights, the fans, the entire mechanical operation goes dead.

This is what gives permission for others to panic.

The claustrophobic woman raises her arm straight up while breaking into sobs. Seated passengers get to their feet, pressing the ones already standing, so that their fused body pitches back and forth. The man who'd called out the single *No!* resumes shouting it, higher and louder each time.

Lily feels herself being sucked away from the doors. Elbows and shoulders come down on her, forcing her closer to the airless floor. She's halfway there when the screams and bellows cohere to speak the same word.

Quiet!

Enough of them do that the looping announcement coming over the speakers can be heard.

> . . . to please remain calm. We are initiating evacuation procedure. Officers will soon be manually opening the doors. Please follow their instructions and form a line to exit the tunnel at the next station. . . . Attention. We ask you to please remain calm. We are initiating . . .

The struggle toward the doors resumes. Among the cries there's a distinct voice that calls, "There's smoke!" and another that follows with, "It's a *bomb!*" There's no smoke in the car, but the recent memory of such things lifts the frenzy to a new level.

Lily can't remain standing any longer. The bigger men force her under until she's a ball on the floor. She knows this is the way people die in situations like these; the first ones to go down are the first to be trampled. It's certainly harder to breathe where she is. But at least she can see the doors when she couldn't before. And there's relatively more space than when she was standing, so that she manages to crawl between legs.

"A light!" someone shouts, and a second later Lily sees it. The swinging beam of a flashlight outside the car.

The ones behind push harder, so that when the doors open the first half dozen passengers are thrown forward into the dark. It's how Lily ends up at the edge, on hands and knees, her eyes level with a man with a waxed moustache wearing a London Underground uniform.

"One at a time!" he shouts. "You first!"

He slides his hands under Lily's arms and pulls her out. Sets her down and directs his flashlight forward.

"Single file," he says. "Carry on into the next station and up the stairs. Nice and slow."

The ones who had tumbled out of the car are on their feet now too and Lily falls in line behind them. There's only the emergency lights in the walls every twenty yards to see by, but so long as she stays on her feet, she need only feel the back of the passenger ahead to know she's going the right way.

Lily's line joins the one exiting the car ahead of her, and then the one ahead of that. They shuffle around what seems a never-ending bend. The cries are only more haunting in the near-dark, echoed by the walls in a way that makes it impossible to tell if they come from behind or ahead.

Eventually the brighter oval of the Goodge Street station reveals itself, the posters on the station walls advertising skin cream and a footballer's memoir bringing an odd comfort.

Lily wonders if Will is ahead or behind her.

She's on the platform now, where she joins a crowd inching closer to the escalators. The passengers are calmer here, reassured by the familiarity of the fluorescent lights just as she had been.

But something's still wrong, Lily tells herself again.

And then she sees she's right.

There's an explosion of movement on the platform ahead. Someone fighting to get through, coming at her. First a man and then a woman are pushed off the platform to make way, the two of them hitting the concrete hard and crumpling into heaps between the rails.

Black Parka.

He spots her at the same time she spots him.

She scans for a way out. There's nothing she can do except push back the way she came but it's as useless as trying to hold back an oncoming tide with your hands.

Black Parka is twenty feet away when his expression changes. He draws a pistol from inside his jacket. Aims it not at her but at something he sees behind her.

"Lily!"

She swings around to find Michael charging toward her through the tunnel. Throwing people aside, cutting a path in front of him. In the dimness she can see the flash of the blades extending past the ends of his fingers, the silver points of his teeth.

"Lily! Run!"

As Michael pulls free of the people at the front of the train he bounds along the tracks into the blue light of the station.

Darkness.

Lily is suffocating in it. The air around her stifling and thin.

Something is holding her but she gets a hand free long enough to grab at the hood covering her head before Black Parka wrenches her arm down to join the other behind her back.

He drags her behind him, the heels of her boots scraping along the platform floor.

"Michael!" she calls out.

Black Parka releases her and she falls to her knees. It takes a second to pull the hood off, but it's still fast enough to look up and see Michael plunge a clawed hand into Black Parka's stomach.

Michael glances down at her to make sure she's watching, a teacher imparting an important lesson. With a pull straight up he draws the blades through the spaces between the man's ribs all the way to his chin before extracting the claws from his neck. A motion that's followed a full second later by a heaving disgorgement of blood.

Black Parka stares down at his gutted torso in disbelief. As if merely curious, he at first watches the parts of him that had been inside his body spill out onto his shoes. His hands reach for them, trying to pull them back in. He turns his head to Lily, his face seeming to ask how things could have come to this. As he falls he keeps his eyes on her. He's dead by the time he collapses onto his side.

"There's more of them," Michael says, and picks her up with one arm.

Lily watches the crowd part as they run straight into it. With the back of his free hand Michael knocks people down, cutting others as he swings it in front of him. The slashing claw moving so fast it's as if blurred propeller blades power them forward.

"Hold on to me," he says.

She wraps her arms around his middle and links her fingers together, locking herself to him.

Lily becomes aware of the screaming. It comes from the passengers close enough to see what Michael is doing—what he's just done. An impossible being doing impossible things before their eyes.

They make it to the base of the escalator. There's more people on the stairs, and even though some of them press themselves against the railings to let them pass, the way up is a moving slope of bodies, jolting and spinning with panic. Michael chooses the escalator. Once people see the decision he's made, several of the ones higher up start to climb over the metal median to get out of their way, rolling onto the stairs, bowling people over and sending them down to plow into other legs, an avalanche of limbs and screeching mouths.

Michael is twenty feet up when he's hit.

Lily feels the impact against his chest, so close to her linked hands it feathers air against her fingers. A bullet. Michael barely slows, his legs pausing for the length of a hiccupped gasp before he carries on, clutching a man ahead of him by the belt and throwing him back over his shoulder. Lily watches the man tumble down the escalator, leaving strings of blood in the grooves of the steps.

"Stop!"

It's Will. Breaking through the line of people below and aiming a gun up at them.

He wasn't the one who shot Michael. That came from above. But Lily can see how Will lines up his aim, ready to fire. His only hesitation comes from trying to find a part of Michael's body that won't also strike hers.

Will starts up after them. Michael glances back and fights his way higher again.

The escalator stops. Someone must have hit the emergency button because there's an alarm now, an old-fashioned bell of the kind that used to summon Lily back into school from hiding alone on the playgrounds of her youth.

They're two-thirds of the way up when Michael's hit again. Another shot to the chest, this one on the left to match the one on the right.

Lily spots the shooter, a man with the same kind of gun that Will holds, his face familiar. It's the taxi driver who'd taken her to the Lipótmezei asylum. Not a taxi driver at all but one of the hunters. Now hunting her and Michael.

Taxi Driver fires again and finds Michael's shoulder just under the collarbone.

He didn't slow after the first two hits, but now he falters, listing one way and then the other, scraping Lily along the side of the escalator, nearly pulling her free. He manages to bring her up so that he holds her like a child being carried to bed.

At this angle Lily sees Michael wasn't shot by bullets, but darts—their ends, marked red by tiny feathers, sticking out from their points of impact. She remembers Will saying that one of them would likely kill a man. But even with three in him, Michael keeps climbing. She looks into his face, his eyes rolling in their sockets, fighting to hold their focus. His lips are trembling, attempting to speak.

"Did you?" she hears him say.

She understands the words that would follow if he could summon them.

Did you tell them?

She looks away, as clear an admission as if she'd said yes. Yet he still doesn't let her go.

Will is an arm's length away from them now. He hasn't shot for fear of hitting Lily, but now she's out of the way, leaving Michael's back exposed. There's the briefest hesitation when he meets her eyes and sees the rage in them, the dawning realization of how this was all set up and how she hadn't been told of it, how his goals are not what he claimed them to be, before he shoots a dart between Michael's shoulder blades.

At the landing, Michael collapses onto Lily. She can neither move nor breathe. A second later, Will and Taxi Driver are pulling him off her.

"You okay?" Will asks her.

"Fucking *liar!*"

Two other men join them. Together with Taxi Driver, they lift Michael up.

"Move!" one of them is shouting at the passengers standing in their way. "Anti-terror! Step aside! *Anti-terror!*"

They wear no uniforms or identification but everyone believes them. It's why, when the real police come at them and Will's men bring out handguns, they're startled to see them take down two officers with shots to the forehead. Their fall is the last thing Lily sees before Will pulls a hood from his jacket and slips it over her head. The two policemen folding to their knees in unison like modern dancers, a synchronized violence that ends with them smacking their skulls on the stone floor.

Now it's Will who carries her. She writhes and kicks and tries to scream, but her struggles feel pillowed, her voice stolen by the limited air inside the hood. Any second she expects to be shot the same way the police were. That's what they're going to do, here or somewhere else, she's sure of it. This might be the last few moments of her life and what's almost as bad as the horror of that is her inability to figure out the chain of events that brought her to this place.

There's shrieking and new alarms to join the ringing bell and then all of it is sucked away. By the lack of an echo to their footfall Lily judges them to be in a smaller space.

Lily gets lucky. She kicks Will and her foot meets bone hard enough that he drops her.

"The fuck?" she hears Taxi Driver say.

"Hit her," Will says.

Lily braces herself for the bullet. But there's only the bright stab of a needle at the top of her arm.

She feels Will picking her up again. This time,

when she tries to fight him, there's only a spasm, a flailed foot. All of her loose and cold and sick.

Then there is darkness that is darker than the inside of a hood, and she remembers nothing more.

28

"Don't let anything in your head but the one thing," her mother's voice tells her an inch from her ear.

"What thing?"

"The thing you have to do. Because you have to be sure. And once you're sure, don't hesitate."

Lily holds the rifle as still as she can but the barrel moves in a wavering circle no matter how hard she tries to correct it. Her focus shifts between this, her mother's words, the sculpture made of tied-together sticks standing forty yards off among the trees.

More than any of this, it's the feel of her mother next to her that runs through the moment. Her body fused with hers, her strong frame holding her straight like a kind of exoskeleton. Lily has been instructed to feel at one with the gun but she's gone further than that. She is at one with her mother, the Remington, the forest, the earth beneath their knees.

But not the man made of sticks.

That's what it is, not a sculpture at all but a human shape her mother had fashioned out of branches for arms and legs, a square of bark for its chest and mushroom cap for its face. A target.

"I'm ready," Lily says.

"You sure?"

"Yes."

"Then do it."

She instantly regrets it, hates herself for it, but she does what her mother told her not to. She hesitates.

"Do it! *Now,* Lily. Now!"

29

The crack of the gun wakes her from the dream, but it still takes a while for Lily to open her eyes and keep them that way.

A porthole. A glass of white wine. A pair of legs she believes are hers but wearing pants and shoes she doesn't recognize.

"Good morning."

A voice she knows and holds on to, using it like a life preserver that keeps her head above water.

"Where am I?"

Will checks his watch. "Right now? Germany, I would guess."

The porthole is a window that looks out over a

layer of clouds thousands of feet below. The legs are hers, but someone has taken off her clothes and dressed her in new ones. Will holds out a glass of apple juice.

"Drink this," he says. "You need the sugar."

The smell of the juice awakens her thirst. When she's finished she puts the glass down on the table between herself and Will but her numbed fingers knock it over as they retreat.

"It'll take an hour or two to get your motor skills back," he says, righting the glass. "You want something more to drink? Some food? Believe it or not, I've got some pretty good—"

"We're on a plane," she says.

"That's right."

"Where is he?"

"With us."

Lily spins around in her seat and the sudden movement brings black dots swimming before her.

"Easy," Will says, leaning forward to help sit her up straight.

"Is he alive?"

"Yes."

"Asleep?"

"He should be, given how much etorphine we've put in him the last twenty-four hours. He's restrained."

"Restrained," Lily repeats.

He puts his hands on the table in a gesture

261

of full disclosure. "Listen, Lily. I'm sorry for what—"

"Fuck you."

"Let me explain."

"You lied to me. About taking him down on Hampstead Heath, about me being safe. And you're not CIA."

"Would it make any difference if I told you I used to be?"

"Who do you work for?"

"They don't have a name. I'm not sure who funds us specifically, but it's people who've got limitless cash, give or take a billion. We're not government, that's all I'm sure about."

"And these people—they aren't going to use him to save lives."

"No."

"His blood being a cure-all. That was bullshit?"

"Total."

"So *why* then? Why spend all this money on a private army just for him?"

Will glances down at his hands and then back at her. A flash of vulnerability she reads as the real thing.

"They told me it was to kill him," he says.

"But he's still alive."

"We're moving him to another location. He'll be neutralized there."

"Neutralized meaning euthanized?"

"Yes."

"You don't look so certain about that."

Will starts to get up. "I'll get you something to eat. You must—"

"Questions first. *My* questions."

He abandons the weak smile he's been trying to hold since handing her the juice. "Okay," he says, and sits.

"Where are we going?"

"Romania."

"Where precisely?"

"It's probably better if I don't give a specific location."

"Better for you or better for me?"

"Both."

"Why Romania?"

"Money goes further in some places. And you need a lot of money to maintain the kind of privacy we require."

Lily tries to arrange the details circling in her head into a narrative, but some piece slips away just when she's almost got it straight.

Stick to the questions. You're good at those. You'll figure out what the answers mean later.

"Why tell me that story about his blood?" she asks.

"We needed your trust. The idea of him being able to save millions of lives seemed more appealing than assisting a conspiracy to kill him."

"So all that crap about—"

"I don't expect you to believe me, but that's the

263

truth. Along with your protection being my first priority."

"How's that?"

"I was trained to die making sure people in your position are kept safe." He rubs his eyes. "Listen. You'd be dead already if it wasn't for me."

"Michael had plenty of opportunity to hurt me and he didn't."

"I'm not talking about him. I'm talking about us," he says, and Lily remembers Black Parka running after her in Budapest and the Goodge Street platform. "There were members of our team who wanted to take you much earlier, learn what we could, then bury you. I made a case otherwise."

"What do you know about me?"

"You?" he says, as if surprised to have his attention turned to the person in front of him. "I'd say everything except, in my experience, there's always something that people hold on to, no matter how thick the file is."

That's your experience too. Isn't it, Doctor?

"Why is it important that you appear nice to me?"

"It isn't."

Lily resists accepting this, but she does. Despite the blatant lies that have brought her here, she looks at Will's scarred face and even now sees an honest man.

"Go back to the subway," she says.

"It was our plan from the beginning to take him on the Underground," he says.

"Why?"

"To put things on our terms."

"You couldn't have let me in on it?" she says.

"He has a connection to you. You've said so yourself."

"How did you know he'd be on the train?"

"There was a strong probability he would be trailing you from the hotel. And underground we could control the environment—the entries and exits, hacking the computer to stop the train, the lights, the locks."

"Whose call was it?"

"Mine."

"That include murdering two policemen?"

"I wish that didn't have to happen. But I believe in the upside of what we're doing here. Sometimes casualties are part of the collateral damage."

Lily hears this last phrase and recognizes that Michael used the exact same one to describe the lives he'd taken to sustain his own.

"You're the boss of this crew, then," she says. "Must keep you busy. Hunting a monster and playing the white knight with—what would you call me? An asset?"

"It's not like that," he starts. "You have to—"

"How did you shut down the train?" she interrupts him again. "Get us out of the city and onto a private jet? Who can deliver you all that?"

"I already told you. The people I work for have considerable resources."

"And they've chosen to spend them on killing one man."

"Yes."

"Then why is he still alive?"

Will pauses at this and she immediately knows he's asked himself the same thing. His hesitation reveals a doubt he didn't have before.

"I have orders to deliver him to them first," he says finally.

"So they can do what? Let him talk to a chaplain? Order his last meal before strapping him in the chair?"

"I think there's some of them who'd like to see the quarry they've spent so much on capturing."

"That doesn't make a lot of sense. There must be another reason."

"Maybe. But they sign the checks."

One of Will's men walks past to step into the lavatory at the front of the plane. Lily recognizes him. The handsome man drinking outside the pub near the Montague Hotel, the one who called out to her. *One on me, luv!* Before he closes the door he looks back at her and winks.

"Why am I here?" she asks.

Will rubs at the stubble along his jawline.

"I'm sorry," he says. "But you can appreciate the importance of confidentiality in an operation like this."

"You can't keep me. People back home will know I'm missing."

"No, they won't. You know that better than anyone. You left your life behind. And now you're gone."

"Who are you?" she says.

"What do you mean?"

"Who. Are. You. It's pretty simple. I'd like to know why the person who's kidnapped me is doing what he's doing."

The lavatory door opens and the man from the pub comes out. Will waits for him to pass before speaking in a lowered voice.

"I've been trained in many skills, but none more important than not existing."

"But you do. You're right here."

"I'm here," he says, as if he needs to talk himself into it.

Lily is trying to think of another way to get him to open up when there's the sound of growling from somewhere behind her. She gets up and stands in the aisle, looking for him.

They've put him in a chair at the very back of the plane. It's one designed specifically for him: thick leather straps around his ankles, legs, waist, chest, even his neck. He still wears his hood so Lily can't see his face, but she can imagine it. It's the sound he's making. A low roar vibrating through the floor.

Whatever the hell that is, it's not Michael, she tells herself. *His body. But not him.*

A man and woman Lily hasn't seen before stand near him, one on each side. The woman holds a syringe, the man a gun.

"When you die . . . I'll be waiting . . ."

A voice like grinding stone comes from inside the hood. A shuddering bass that hits Lily square in the chest.

The woman plunges the needle in. Lily expects Michael to roar again, but he does something worse. He laughs. A sound that is nothing like him.

And it's not one voice but the laughter of dozens, women and men and children. A noise that grows louder until the tranquilizer takes effect and the voices disappear, one by one, until there's just one left: a girl's. And she's not laughing now, but crying.

Lily's heard it before. She tries to remember who it belongs to and realizes it's her.

30

Lily devours a stale cheese sandwich and knocks back a liter of apple juice before the plane lands on a cracked airstrip surrounded by barbed wire fence and, squeezed against it, a wall of knotted shrubs.

Will sits across from her again. He looks even more ragged than earlier. Fatigue has reddened the grooves in his skin, speckled his face with the beginnings of a gray beard.

"Almost there," he says.

"What's there?"

"The physical base of operations. Along with a room for the guest of honor."

The plane bumps to a halt on the tarmac. Through the window, Lily can see no sign of an outbuilding or vehicle or any other aircraft. They could be anywhere but for the low, charcoal clouds she now associates with Eastern Europe.

"Are you going to put that hood on me again?" she asks.

"Don't need to. And I have to trust you sometime, right?"

"Otherwise you'll never let me go."

"If you want to put it that way, yeah."

It occurs to Lily once again that she may not survive to the end of the day. Somehow she'd assumed she was outside of things, immune, an informant who would be free to go once the job was done. This belief was based on her relationship with Will as much as wishful thinking.

"How long am I going to be here?"

"I don't know. There's a few things I need to secure first," he says. "And then I have to figure out a cover for you."

"A cover?"

"Where you've been the last few days. Who you've seen and why. If someone asks you about any of this, you need to have airtight responses, and we need to back them up on the records. Shall we go?"

"I need a drink."

"More juice?"

"A real drink."

"Come with me."

On the tarmac there's a banged-up older model Mercedes and VW van in almost worse shape waiting for them.

"The budget doesn't cover airport limos?" she says as Will opens the back door of the Mercedes for her.

"This is Romania. New cars get noticed," he says. "And this isn't an airport."

He gets in next to her and the car rattles off past an unmanned security hut. Soon they're on a two-lane road that takes them through fields that appear to be growing stones and a couple of villages with only a handful of stout, kerchief-headed women on the sidewalks.

She tries to remind herself that, at any moment, the driver may take a turn onto a quieter lane and Will will apologize, but she has to get out now, that it will go easier if she cooperates and doesn't make any noise. It frightens her, but not as much as she would have guessed. So many other unreal things have happened to her over the last handful of days that the possibility of her own death feels like one more unsettling event among others. She can sustain this sense of distance so long as the car keeps going and doesn't slow and turn.

And then the car slows and turns.

They bump along a rutted drive and into a broad woodlot with tight lines of planted pines on both sides. There's no sign that they're getting any closer to what may pass for a "physical base of operations." Only the trees and the forest floor, a brown carpet of fallen needles.

"Almost there," Will says, just as he had on the plane.

After several hundred yards the Mercedes comes to a stop. Ahead of them are two high fences running parallel. Bundles of razor wire lie in the space between the two. The road they're on runs directly into them and, before part of the first fence and then the other starts to open, Lily saw no way of getting inside.

They drive through and into a paved square with several single-story cement buildings. Grass grows through the cracks in the pavement. Crude graffiti the only decoration on the walls.

The car drives to one of the buildings and a garage door is rolled up. Inside it's dark. All the darker when the door closes behind them.

"Right this way," Will says, getting out of the car.

Lily follows him to a door where he enters a security code in a panel. Beyond it there's a fluorescent-lit stairway that descends farther than she can see.

Will starts down and Lily is behind him. She looks back to see if the driver or anyone else joins them but the door swings shut, leaving them alone.

The descent takes long enough for her to feel the wrongness of being underground at this depth and in a tunnel this small. Just as the cold perspiration begins to dampen her clothes they reach the bottom and start down a long hallway with a number of metal doors on either side. Lily looks past Will to see where it ends. Fifty yards on there's a wall where the hall splits and carries on in both directions. The subsequent turns and breaks that follow put Lily in the mind of a maze, one that starts out simply but compounds in difficulty the closer you try to come to its center.

Will opens a door onto a narrower hallway with still more doors off it. He chooses one and steps inside. It reminds Lily of a holding cell at the Kirby: a single bed, a desk, a standing closet.

"This is my room," he says. "You can have the one at the end. Bathroom is on the other side. If you're planning on a shower, I'd lock the door. These guys down here are professionals, but I can't vouch for all of them."

Will pulls a bottle of Maker's Mark out of the desk drawer, pours them each a generous shot, and Lily drinks half of hers down.

"I have a request," she says.

"Okay."

"I want to speak with him."

Will ponders this. "I don't see why not," he says. "But I don't see *why* either."

"He was my client once, remember? The doctor in me likes to close her files."

He finishes his drink in a gulp. "Whatever you want, Dr. Dominick. But now, if you wouldn't mind, I've got some calls to make. I'll knock later."

Lily leaves and goes to her room at the end of the hall. She thinks that this may be her only opportunity to come up with a plan, a way of escape. But whether it's the bourbon or the effects of being knocked out for so long she lies down on the bed and closes her eyes. Sleep curls around her like a cat. She's about to give herself over to it when she jolts up.

He's here.

There's no sound other than the buzzing of the light in her room, no change in temperature or smell. But she senses his arrival all the same. Somewhere within the underground labyrinth the minotaur has been placed in his cell.

He's here. But it's not him anymore.

Her intuition tells her that dreaming is dangerous, especially when a spirit like his wants you, is searching for you. But she can't resist and falls asleep anyway.

Almost instantly she dreams of a knock at the door. The knob turns on its own, the door slowly swings open. It's Will.

A pointed tongue comes out of his twisted mouth and lengthens as far as his waist. But when he speaks it's in the demon's voice.

I've tasted you. But now it's time to eat . . .

31

When she wakens Will is sitting at the end of her bed.

"Things have changed," he says. He looked tired before. Now he's worried.

She sits up on her elbows. "What things?"

"The people I work for, this whole mission—it wasn't what I was led to believe."

"You need to be a bit more specific."

"My job was to bring the man you call Michael to this place so he could be exterminated. I've done that. But now they're telling me they're on their way here. Not just the money men. Scientists, surgeons. In a couple days this place is going to be transformed into a research facility."

"Studying him?"

"They want to know how he's been able to live for two hundred years without aging. They haven't been funding us to remove a threat from the world. They've been after the one and only fountain of youth."

"You've been misled."

"Fucking right I've been misled."

"It never occurred to you that was what they were after all along?"

"Believe it or not, it didn't. I only saw what I wanted to see, which was to see him dead."

"Why did you want that so badly?"

"You don't understand. I sought these people out. I needed them to kill him. It couldn't be done on my own. I know because I tried."

"Why?" Lily asks again. It brings Will closer.

"He killed my sister," he says.

32

"Tell me," Lily says.

Will wipes his hand over his mouth and Lily sees that both his hands and lips are trembling.

"It was a Friday night," he says. "Me and Amanda went to see the nine o'clock showing of *The Usual Suspects*. We were walking home and I got the feeling we were being followed. Everyone in Madison—that's where we lived—was talking about the missing persons cases that had hit the papers that week. A student last seen walking across campus, a mother of two who didn't return from a drive downtown to pick up a new pair of glasses. It made people nervous.

"We could see our house on the far side of the playground, the lights on in the kitchen, the TV on. Our mother was waiting up. Just a quick walk up the lane to the front, or a climb over the backyard fence, and we'd be home. It didn't make me feel any better. So I made Amanda an offer. If she beat me home I'd give her twenty bucks. A race. I even gave her a five-second head start. *Bam!* She was gone. And I was counting. Five . . . four . . . three. On two I saw it."

Will squints into the middle distance and Lily can see how he's there. Back to the night when everything shattered and couldn't be put together again.

"A figure rising up from the little bridge connecting the jungle gym to the slide. Amanda didn't even see it. I tried to run to catch up to her but my feet wouldn't move. There was this invisible hand on my chest, pushing against me. Something that made me watch as the figure took its time sitting down at the end of the bridge and sliding down the slide."

Will shifts his gaze to Lily. It lets her see how his eyes have blurred with tears. Not grief, but rage.

"I called out to her but the hand on my chest pushed so much of the air out of my lungs I couldn't speak. The figure stood up. I could see its long fingers now. Pointed and hooked. Amanda was even with it when she almost tripped. The thing must have said something. She watched it come closer, taking its time. I was screaming but it was only in my head. *Amanda! Come back!* I had to get to her. And to do that, I had to tell myself that the invisible hand holding me there wasn't real. The thing had *suggested* it was, but it was my mind alone that had frozen me. And I was in charge of my mind. Me. Not the thing that put its clawed hand on my sister's shoulder."

Will swallows. Sits up straight. Breathes in the strength it takes to tell what happened next.

"I broke free. Sprinting right at them. Even as

I got closer and she came into focus the thing—it went for her throat. I remember her face. No pain, just this kind of disappointment, like she'd expected to win a contest but had learned the prize had been given to someone else. When I hit the playground's sand it slowed me a notch. I was so close I thought there was still time to tackle the thing—I never thought of it as a man, not once—and pull it away. But as soon as I was close enough it swung the back of its hand at me. It spun my head around so hard I thought it was going to rip clean off. And the claws—the points met my face before I went down. That thing did this to me."

He touches his face without thinking, his fingertips playing over the marks as if he were a blind man reading Braille.

"When I landed it was on the metal edge at the bottom of the slide, the sharp edge slicing through the top of my arm," he goes on. "I was close to passing out, could feel it inside me like a chemical smoke. But I could still watch the thing feeding on my sister. Her eyes on mine for the last moments of her life so that I witnessed her passing without being able to give her any comfort. When it was done, it dropped her onto the sand like a bag of garbage. It looked at me. *Remember.* I told myself that over and over. *Remember its face.* And I did. Every crease in its lips as it opened them to speak. 'Honey sweet,' it said."

33

I gave the police a description and they drew up a composite," Will says a moment later, after Lily offers him her hand and he takes it. "It looked like the thing on the surface but wasn't him. They turned an *it* into a *him,* know what I mean?"

" 'Something wrong with his appearance; something displeasing, something downright detestable . . . He gives a strong feeling of deformity, although I couldn't specify the point,' " Lily says.

"What's that?"

"It's from *Dr. Jekyll and Mr. Hyde.*"

"Yeah? Well that pretty much nails it."

Lily is about to tell Will about Michael's journal, his encounters with Shelley, Stoker, and Stevenson, maybe even the blood relationship between herself and him. She wants to offer something in return for what he's just shared with her, but decides to hold on to it. There's value in what she knows, which makes it the only thing she has to bargain with.

"Why not do it now?" Lily says. "Kill him. Before they get here."

"Because they'd kill me. If that was all, I'd

still do it. But they'd also kill you. And I'm not having that on my head."

He pulls away his hand and places it on her leg. The heat of it stops the shiver that had started at the base of her spine. Part of her wonders if he's about to venture his hand higher and is surprised to find that part of her wants him to. But she knows that's not what this is about. He's using her as an anchor.

"What are you going to do?"

"Make sure you're safe," he says. "I'd get you out of here right now but that would be more dangerous than convincing them to agree to it."

"What would you say the odds of that is?"

"Fifty-fifty."

"I want to see him."

Will lifts his hand away. "Why?"

"If things go bad for me, I want to speak to him before they do."

"What could you say that would make any difference?"

"He's here because of me," she says. "When he thought your men were going to kill me in the subway it brought him out into the open. He tried to save me."

"Why do you think that is?"

"I don't know," Lily lies. "Maybe that's why I want to see him."

Will doesn't move. It could be that he's making

the same calculations about betting on her as she has just done about him.

"Okay," he says, abruptly standing. "The zoo is this way."

34

She follows him to the end of the hall they first entered after coming down the stairs. The doors they pass are marked only by letters and numbers in seemingly random order—T-432 followed by E-896—so they couldn't be used to mark an advance or retreat. They make a left, a right, and another right before she realizes she'll never remember the way they've come and gives up trying.

Eventually Will opens a door that looks like all the others and the two of them enter a grimy room smelling of fried hamburger. There's a table with a single laptop on it. Will closes the door and goes to stand next to a control panel set into the wall.

"Ready?"

Lily isn't sure what he's asking, but she nods anyway.

Will turns a dial on the controls and a rectangle of light appears on the wall farthest from the door. When her eyes adjust, she can see it's a window, one that looks into a room on the other side.

There's more furnishings in this room, all of them suggestive of a maximum-security asylum combined with a surgical theater. A gurney with leather and metal restraints hanging over the sides, an exposed toilet in the corner. No mirror, no sink, no bed.

Lily approaches the glass and sees the monster.

It sits in the middle of the bare floor, rocking back and forth, its eyes on the door. As she watches, its head slowly turns. When it finds her through the glass, it stops, the eyes held on her.

"Can it see me?" she asks.

"No. Can't hear us either unless I turn the speaker on."

"Then why is it staring right at me?"

Will waves at the creature, knocks at the glass, but it doesn't blink. "I don't know," he says. "You could detonate a grenade in here and you wouldn't hear it where it is."

Lily raises a hand and places it against the glass. It brings the creature to its feet, though it takes several seconds to do it. Its body rearranges itself as it rises, an assembling of parts like a broken doll stitching itself together. When it stands, Lily sees for certain it's not Michael anymore. The skin is the skin she'd touched, the face comprised of the same features. But this thing is no more her father than a stranger who'd stolen his coat.

"Can I speak to it?"

"Be my guest," Will says, and turns the

two-way sound on, the volume up so high the two of them listen to the thing's wet breaths on the other side. Then they see it too: a long string of yellow spit stretching from his lower lip before it breaks away to slap onto the floor.

"You," the thing says.

A single word that frightens her more than any sound she's ever heard. A voice embodied by the shoulders slanted to one side, the spine bent into an S. The forward thrust of its head and snap of its mouth with every step forward.

"Honey sweet."

Lily turns to Will and sees the fury these words provoke in him. But the anger is instantly smothered by something greater, the fear that comes with finally meeting the nightmare from his childhood and being a stricken child again.

It turns to face Will through the glass. "My little girl," it says.

Until now, Lily has seen only one side of Michael. The hunched creature in front of her is the other half, the thing that emerged from Dr. Edmundston's kitchen, the monster that tore her mother to pieces. The demon Robert Louis Stevenson named Hyde.

"I want to speak to Michael," Lily says.

The thing looks around, trying to find where her voice is coming from. It's been a while since it's been in charge of the body it inhabits, and it's getting used to the world all over again. When its eyes land once more on the rectangle of one-way glass Lily stands behind, it freezes on her. Its face contorting into an expression of agony, though something about it tells her it's an attempt at a smile.

"Your voice," it says. "You will sing so sweetly when I make you scream."

"I'm not interested in you. I want to speak to Michael."

It steps closer to the glass, the twisted smile dropping away.

"He's dead," it says. "He's *always* been dead."

"I'm not afraid of you."

"You should be."

"You forget that I work with psychotics for a living. There's no profanity or threat I haven't already heard."

"But you know I will do what I say I will do. And you know I am not one of your psychotics."

Lily has to force herself not to pull away from the glass. She glances over at Will. He motions toward the button that will cut off the speaker but Lily shakes her head no.

"Look around," she says, returning her gaze to the thing. "You're the one in a cage."

The thing does as she says. It looks around the cell and utters a single bark of laughter.

"*This* is my cage?"

"They will torture you in there. You'll feel what you've done to others for once."

It raises one of its hands for Lily to see and takes the forefinger and thumb of the other hand to grip the index finger's nail. Lily can hear the sound of the nail slowly pulled back, ripping away from the skin.

"Fun," it says, flicking the nail against the glass inches from Lily's face.

"An empty show," she manages. "It's over."

"But I have such great plans for us."

"If you can get out, why don't you?"

"That would ruin the surprise."

Lily slides to the right and the thing's eyes follow her. If it could break through the barrier between them it already would have. But with every passing moment she weakens, it gains in strength.

"Are you feeling all right, daughter?" it says. She has to look away and fight to swallow hot bile before she can speak again.

"Are you Peter Farkas?" she asks.

"I am no one."

"But you remember him, don't you?"

"I remember *all* of them. Their eyes and hearts and assholes and cocks. Their pain."

The thing leans closer to the glass until its nose and lips are pressed against it, the pink flesh whitened at the points of contact.

"And now . . . you live in Michael," Lily says in a broken whisper.

"No Peter. No Michael."

The thing's voice is in the observation room with her, filling the space so that there is nothing but its words. Even the smell of its breath has seeped through to the other side.

"You'll see this for yourself," it says. "I promise no names will come to you. No language. No prayer."

Lily motions for Will to turn off the sound and darken the glass. In her peripheral vision she sees him trying to do just that but he's in a hold of some kind, his hands gnarled into arthritic hooks that won't do what he asks.

The demon speaks so low it's as if its words rise up from the earth below.

"I can already taste you. Soon—"

Will's hand smacks against the control panel and hits the audio button. The thing still speaks but the observation room's speakers don't let the sound pass through. It doesn't matter. Lily can hear it all the same.

Soon you'll be inside me and I'll be inside you.

"Turn off the light," Lily tells Will.

"I'm trying. My hands—"

"Turn off the *light!*"

Will turns the dial with his palm and the window darkens.

For a second, even when it's black as the bottom of a well, the thing's face remains visible. The whites of its eyes. Its teeth.

35

The fuck was that?"

Will rubs his hands and looks to Lily with the same bewildered expression many of the lawyers gave her when visiting their clients for the first time at the Kirby.

The thing Dr. Eszes made Michael out of.

A serial killer named Peter Farkas who died in the early nineteenth century.

A devil.

"I don't really know," she says.

"It was *holding* me."

"Michael can do that too, but he's not as strong as the thing in there."

Will shakes his arms as if trying to throw off invisible ropes still binding them.

"Are you saying he has a split personality?"

"It's more than that. There are two beings in the same body," Lily answers. "One is the thing we just saw. The other is a man—something less and more than a man—who was brought to life over two hundred years ago."

"Brought to life," he repeats. "You mean a resuscitation? A reanimated corpse?"

"He's not the same thing who occupied the body in life. He's something new. No conception.

No childhood, no growing up. No father, no mother, no family, no home."

Now that she's said this out loud a sadness comes over Lily. Most of it in sympathy for the thing she calls Michael, but also for herself. If he has proceeded out of nothing it confirms what she's always felt, that some of her is unknown to herself as well.

"He's told you all this?" Will asks.

"Some of it. And some of it he's wanted me to discover. He wants me to answer for him the same things you're asking of me."

"You got a working theory?"

"I've wondered if he's a stray soul who found an opportunity to live again in another's skin," she says, speaking aloud a thought she's barely entertained before now.

"Whose soul?"

"I don't know. Even he doesn't know. He's searching for his name. An identity. It's part of why he came to me."

"Is that what he was saying about 'my daughter'?"

"Yes."

"Yes what?"

She takes a step back from the glass as if the thing in the darkness is still there, listening.

"Yes," she says. "Michael is my father."

36

Will and Lily make their way back to her room and resume their positions on the bed—she lying propped up at the waist, he seated at the foot—and look at each other for a time as if to confirm they're both there, both witnesses to what they've just experienced, to the confession she's just made.

"Are there any more of you?" Will asks finally, breaking the silence. "I mean, does he have any more children?"

"He's told me I'm the only one, and I believe him."

"What's he want from you?"

"To not be alone."

Will is about to ask something more when the radio attached to his belt awakens with a burst of static. Buried in the white noise is a voice they both recognize as the man who stood outside the bar in London. His sentences broken by the poor reception.

. . . situation . . . rumpel . . . jeopardy . . .

"These walls down here—they're old-school bombproofed," Will says, pulling the radio up to his ear. "Sure as hell messes with reception."

"What's 'rumpel'?"

"The code we use for the target. Short for

Rumpelstiltskin." Will presses a button at the side of the radio. "Leader One here. Say again, over."

Another round of crackling, only one word making its way through.

"I heard 'opening,' " Lily says.

"Me too."

The hunter Lily had seen outside the London pub watches the man in the cell hurt himself.

Even though she's not there, Lily can see it happening. The demon has reached into her mind and is letting her watch. *Making* her watch.

The hunched thing stands two feet away, pounding its head into the glass. Its skull and the hard surface meet in a series of cracks that leave a dripping circle of blood.

The hunter lifts the radio held in his hand.

"Leader One? We've got a situation here," he says into the mouthpiece. "Rumpel is in jeopardy."

He doesn't go any closer to the door. It's not hesitation but a kind of enchantment with the sight of the man repeatedly smashing his head. Something impossible to understand that he struggles to figure out like those children's puzzles where you have to spot the distinctions between two seemingly identical pictures. What's different about this man and any other man? The hunter decides it's the look on his face. His eyes meeting the hunter's even though it isn't possible for the latter to be seen. The grin that doesn't falter as its open mouth lets in the freely flowing blood from the widening wound at the top of its forehead.

He tries the radio again.

"Leader One? You getting this, over?"

There may be words of reply in the noise, but the hunter steps toward the door without waiting to hear them, the decision not his anymore, but a command from the thing on the other side.

Open the door.

Will is at Lily's door when he stops to look back at her. "You coming?"

Lily gets off the bed so fast that her head feels like it might float off her neck. She fights it, her hands out at her sides like a tightrope walker's.

Will starts down the hall at a run, pulling his gun from its holster. At the corner he looks back to make sure she's behind him.

"You have to *run!*"

As Lily runs, the monster shows her how the hunter dies.

He exits the observation room and slips around the corner into the antechamber outside the target's cell, passing a table on which its cracked leather gloves with blades for fingers and set of metal teeth are laid. Through a small window in the door he can see that the man on the other side is no longer pounding his head against the one-way glass. He's standing in the center of the room, his clothes covered with thickening red like a human candle, his hair a matted wick atop his head.

"Don't move," the hunter says, entering the code that opens the door. It reminds him to pull the tranq gun out of his back pocket.

For a moment time slows so that the candle man is there, the hunter lifting the gun as if it's attached to sacks of sand. And then the candle man is right in front of him. Pulling the gun out of the hunter's hand and dropping it to the floor.

Breathe in, the candle man says.

Will takes so many turns and is so much faster that Lily imagines a line between them, a jump rope, like the ones she and her classmates held on to on school field trips. So long as she can feel it between them she doesn't worry about getting lost, only moving her legs.

He stops to open a door next to the observation room they were in only minutes ago. She stays in the hall as Will enters the anteroom outside the cell. From where she is she can see the gurney, the toilet in the corner. That's when she realizes she shouldn't be able to see these things if the cell's door was closed.

"We should go," she says.

But Will isn't listening. She follows his line of sight and finds the London pub hunter on the floor, his body holding the cell door open, the arms and legs splayed out as if they had attempted to slow his fall from a great height. Next to it is the hunter's head. It looks at Lily with a horror similar to her own.

"He's not here," Will is saying to her from miles away. He lays his hands on the sides of her face and makes her look at him.

"He's not here," Will says again. "Which means I have to get you out. Understand?"

Before Lily can nod there's a gunshot. A single, useless pop, followed by a man's scream.

"Now," Will says.

37

Will looks behind him every few yards as they run. His eyes so wild she reads them as meaning the thing is gaining on them, but she never looks back to confirm it.

While they don't hear any more gunshots, there's another scream. Different from the one before. It tells Lily the first shot didn't bring the thing down. It also tells her the second screaming man didn't have time to draw his weapon.

She waits to hear the monster's howling or laughter over her own strangled breaths, and a moment later she *does* hear both these things, though she can't tell if it's of her own imagining. It may not make a difference anymore. To imagine it is to make it real. To hear it is to let it in.

Will opens a door midway along a hallway longer than the others. She follows him inside and sees that it's an office: a metal desk, single filing cabinet, a chair with its stuffing bursting out of holes.

"Take this," Will says, swinging around to hand her his gun. She holds it in her palm like a bird with a broken wing. "Stand at the door and make sure nothing's coming."

Lily positions herself a few inches past the doorframe, checks both ways. Thirty feet to the right a fluorescent tube flickers in its death spasm, throwing irregular shadows over the floor.

Behind her, Will pulls a large envelope and a handheld device out of the drawer. When he turns it on, it emits an awakening beep and a screen illuminates. He studies it before smacking its side.

Lily spins around. "What's wrong?"

"We put a locator chip in him when he was knocked out," Will says. "This should tell us where he is, but it doesn't work down here any better than the radios."

She checks the hallway again. The light tube is

strobing now, so that for a millisecond, she thinks she can see the thing that isn't Michael in a band of darkness. But with the next blink of light it disappears.

"What now?" she asks.

"We get out."

"Which way?"

"Right or left. You choose."

Lily gives the gun back to him and starts to the left, away from the fluorescent tube that turns black with a pop.

"This way," she says.

Lily feels the maze consuming her, pulling her deeper to where the minotaur awaits.

Hallways and doors with maddening numbers and letters on them, on and on. Will hesitates more than once when choosing between the routes to take, which makes her believe he's only guessing now.

Every turn they make she's certain it will be there, grinning at the ease with which they had come to it on their own. It's why, when Will abruptly stops in front of a door that looks like all the others, she thinks it's to say it's over, there's no way out.

"Here," he says, opening the door to a lit passage and starting up the narrow stairs inside.

Half a dozen steps up and they're swallowed by darkness again. Lily hears Will pounding upward ahead of her, the distance widening between them. She tells herself to stop feeling for her footing and just trust she won't fall. The ascent warms the air as they go until it's stifling. She considers pausing to steady herself but hears movement at the base of the stairs behind her, something sliding over the concrete, and she keeps leaping blindly forward.

When the light hits her it knocks her back. It *hits* her—the paleness of the outside, the gray revelation of the stairwell, her own swaying body.

"We've got to go," Will tells her from the top. He's holding the GPS device and it's making sounds now. A pulse of beeps so close together it echoes the panicked drumroll of her heart.

She uses her arms to start up again. Swinging them at her sides to launch herself into motion.

"See that car over there?" Will says, pointing at one of the beat-up Mercedes parked forty yards away and slapping a set of keys into her palm. "Get in the driver's seat."

"What about you?"

He points the gun down the stairwell where the light reaches halfway before yielding to the dark.

"I'm making sure you have time to start it," he says.

Lily heads toward the car but not before detecting the smell of the thing. The spoiled meat of its breath drifting up from the stairs.

She pulls on the car's door handle and falls into the seat.

"I'm in!" she shouts back at Will as she turns the key and the engine rattles and knocks. But he's not looking her way. He's frozen by something coming up at him from underground.

Lily considers running back, shaking him, when she hears the crisp pop of his gun.

"Will!"

Her voice reaches him this time. He turns, sees her in the car. Puts one foot in front of the other until he's sprinting her way.

"Did you get him?" she asks once he lands in the passenger seat next to her.

"I'm not sure."

"But you saw him?"

"I heard him."

"What did he say?"

Will almost tells her, but shakes his head free of the words. "Drive," he says.

Lily hits the gas. They're moving, taking the corner around one of the compound's out-buildings and toward the fence.

"This is Leader One," Will shouts into the radio. "Control? Open the gate."

She doesn't slow even though the fence remains in place.

"Control! Open the gate!"

Will has leaned forward to look into the mirror

on the passenger door. It prompts Lily to do the same in the rearview.

The thing comes around the corner.

Still hunched, its strides irregular, but moving incredibly fast, charging toward their car like a hybrid of animal and insect. Gorilla, spider, bull.

Lily looks forward again and sees the two gates of the interior and exterior fences slowly pulling open. There's no way it will be wide enough by the time they reach it.

"Go. Go. *Go,*" Will is saying.

Lily angles the car into a head-on approach, aiming straight through the gap. A second before impact, she checks the rearview again. Sees the monster barreling closer, its eyes fixed on hers.

They make it through the first fence but the second clips the driver's side, sending the car fishtailing. Will pushes her up straight and she corrects the skid, the Mercedes bucking over the road's hardened mounds.

Lily is no longer driving. She holds her foot down hard on the gas and grips the wheel, that's all.

Her attention is fixed on the thing that isn't Michael. Coming through the opened gates, uttering a roar she can hear even over the laboring engine.

38

They drive in silence except for Will's directions, a series of turns that takes them through villages so similar Lily is sure they're going in circles.

After they'd driven out of the compound's gates the thing had pursued them for a hundred yards or so before abruptly starting into the forest. For a second it was a bounding interruption through the stillness of the trees, and then it was gone. Will and Lily didn't look at each other for several miles, both of them checking the windows, making sure it didn't come storming out at them.

Now, in one of the villages like all the others, he tells her to pull over in the parking lot outside a convenience store. By the door, a pair of teenaged boys smoke and watch them with the bored attention of a skeptical audience at a magic show.

"Turn off the engine," he says, and the Mercedes shudders before it quiets.

They sit like that for a time, the two of them staring through the windshield at a faded poster for an Iron Maiden concert that happened four years ago.

"You okay?" Will asks.

"I'm not sure how to answer that."

"Neither am I."

She turns to look at him. "Guess your employers aren't going to be very happy," she says.

"No, they won't be. But it's all different now."

"How do you mean?"

"I don't work for them anymore. I don't work for anyone but us."

Lily remembers Will's voice on what she tried to talk herself into being a crank call when she was in New York. *I want to protect you.* Not "we," but "I." This is personal for him, and Lily sees now that it always has been. Tracking Michael, putting an end to him, but also doing for her what he couldn't do for his sister.

Will pulls his gaze away from the poster. "I'm going to hunt it," he says.

"How?"

"Over the time we were tracking Michael we learned more about his operations than he guesses. Where he keeps his caches of money, fake passports. He's out—*it's* out—but he's limited right now. And I've got this," he says, showing the GPS that's emitting a steady, calm series of beeps. "This is the best opportunity I'm ever going to get to find him."

He looks down at his free hand and seems surprised to see that he still holds the gun. Lily waits for him to return it to his holster but he only squeezes it against his thigh, confirming its weight.

"He's going to come for me," she says.

"I know."

"So we should fight it together."

"No."

"Stop being the good soldier for a second. I'm thinking of maximizing our odds, that's all."

"So am I. And we do that by me moving fast and you getting off the field."

He puts the GPS down and fishes from his pocket the envelope he'd taken from the filing cabinet, lays it on her lap.

"What's this?"

"The fail-safe," he says.

Lily tears it open and looks inside. Nestled at the bottom are a USB stick and a single key.

"Once you're out of here, open up the file that's been downloaded on that," he says. "It will give you the location of a safe house and the key will open the door. Inside you'll find weapons, cash, food."

"Where is it?"

"I don't know."

"I'm not following."

Will closes his eyes. "The man who went into the cell, the one it killed—he was someone I'd worked with before. When we started on this we knew it could get sticky, so I prepared a safe house for him and he did the same for me. We didn't tell each other anything about the location so that if one of us fell into the target's

control—or if we disappointed our employers—
we'd have nothing to tell them. I can't give them
your location if I don't know where you are. Not
knowing also protects you from Michael. It's like
you said. Once you're connected to him, he can
reach inside."

"That's true for me. What connects you to
him?"

"My sister. Now you," he says. "Who knows?
Maybe you care a little about me too. That might
be enough."

Lily thinks he's right. Michael could probably
find her by tapping into Will, and vice versa.

She folds the top of the envelope closed.
Outside the window over Will's shoulder the two
teenagers light another round of cigarettes and
wordlessly set to staring at their car again.

"You've laid out all the ways we can't know
where the other is," she says. "What about a way
to be in the same place again?"

"There's a satellite phone at the safe house with
one number on it."

"Yours."

"Yes. But it's not the one you called me with
in London. It's a phone in a location I know but
haven't got to yet," he says. "When you get to
whatever address is on the memory stick, it'll
be up to you whether you call me or not. I'd
understand if you didn't. But if you do, and if I
don't answer, it'll be because I'm dead."

The idea of their parting makes him suddenly more present to her, his body seated so close in the confines of the car that she's alert to even the minutest variations of his heartbeat, the temperature of his skin, his faintly cinnamon breath. Her desire for him is only enhanced by the fear that has stretched her thin ever since she sat across the table from Michael at the Kirby what feels like years ago. She wants to touch this man not to make her fear go away but to enflame it, focus it, invest it with an even more desperate urgency. There are things she wants to do to him. And the notion of doing them now, precisely when she shouldn't want to do them, only sharpens her yearning.

"Yours," he says, handing her an American passport. "You'll need it for the faked visitor visa to Romania. You're not officially here, remember?"

"Right," she says, and opens the booklet to her photo, the exact same stern image that's in her existing passport.

"You'll need access to cash. And some local currency for the bus." He hands her a folded wad of Romanian bills and, wrapped inside it, a bank card with a PIN number taped to the back. "It'll take you to Bucharest. From there, get to the safe house. Do it in multiple transitions so it'll be harder to track you."

Lily pockets the money and looks in the

303

rearview mirror. Nothing there a moment ago but now an ancient passenger bus belching diesel clouds comes leaning around a bend. The two teenagers stub out their cigarettes, saunter across the lot to the bent sign that marks the bus stop.

Lily pulls the handle and her door opens but she doesn't get out. The bus wheezes to a stop at the side of the road and the door opens. The teenagers get on while looking back at her.

"I'll see you," she says, and gets out in a rush.

She boards the bus without looking back and takes a seat on the opposite side from where the Mercedes is parked. All measures she hopes to prevent her from seeing him, from feeling the vacancy he'll leave behind once he's gone. But as the bus squawks into gear she looks out the window and finds him, his smile not quite holding on his face, though for her sake he keeps working at it until the bus rounds the next turn.

39

As Lily bounces along the potholed road through farming crossroads and intermittent patches of forest, she wonders if this is how her mother felt after she'd made the decision that took her to the Alaska cabin. Like her, Lily had sided with the hunters, put her trust in men she didn't really know instead of the one who would do anything to keep her safe.

Was it the right decision that happened to have the wrong outcome? Or should she have chosen Michael from the beginning, recognized that her fate was bound to his no matter what?

What's known is that her mother's decision had left her alone with Lily at the very end of the world. Even though Lily was only six she remembers her mother starting to teach her the things she would need to survive the game she was born into playing. Introducing her to the way to clean and load the .25-06 Remington kept next to the broom by the front door, for one thing. The color of clothes to wear to be camouflaged in the forest at different times of year. The route of the hidden path that led to the rusted trailer down by the creek, what she called the secret place.

Lily assumes it was meant to be where she ought to run and hide if either Michael or the hunters came. She remembers her mother putting boxes in the trailer Lily guessed to contain cans of food and rinsed-out milk jugs of water. It didn't make much sense to her when she thinks of it now: no matter how much food and water was stashed away in the trailer she would have to come out eventually, and where would she go when she did?

"If you see bad things happening, this is where

you go," Lily's mother told her at the trailer door. "You come here without mommy, you come no matter what. Okay?"

Lily wanted to hug her mother instead of listening to this frightening talk but she'd nodded her understanding, even then equating adulthood with the control of one's fears.

After she died, Lily hadn't gone to the trailer but had done precisely what her mother told her not to do and wandered off into the trees. The secret place blotted from her mind by panic, by the images of the monster over her mother's body.

And then the white horse had come.

At the Bucharest airport she chooses a KLM direct flight to Amsterdam for no other reason than it appeared alphabetically first on the departures board. It's night when she arrives. The fear that clings to her, the shifting time zones, the lack of sleep—all of it conspiring to deprive Lily of any sense of the hour. She knows she has to rest or she'll start making bad decisions, and she's made enough of those already.

She takes a room at the Ambassade Hotel in the old city. Even in her condition she registers how lovely this place is, the widening circles of canals she crosses on arched bridges, the young and old on bicycles, the ornate lanterns coloring the streets of stone. It's a fairy-tale city, and as with a fairy tale told before bedtime it helps Lily sleep through the night and most of the next day. She eats in her room, watching the passing boats through her window, reaching her mind out to Will to see if she can sense whether he's found Michael or not, but nothing comes.

The next day she buys a ticket for a flight to New York. She knows there's no way she could return to her apartment, but it's her reflex starting point. It's also where she'll plug in the USB stick Will gave her and find out where the safe house is. She could do the same thing at the airport, but she wants to put at least an ocean between herself and Michael to prevent him from reading her.

When her flight is called she finishes her coffee and drops it along with an issue of the *Guardian* into the recycling bin, the horrors of the wider world too remote to make any sense to her now.

Lily takes her seat in the center row. She immediately closes her eyes. Not falling asleep, just trying to hold on to the sense of escape as the 747 roars down the runway and launches into the sky. It's only when she plugs in the earbuds the flight attendant gives her that she notices it.

An envelope poking out from the magazine pocket in the seat ahead of her. Even after she pulls it out she doesn't open it until the map on the screen shows their position over the North Atlantic. With the idea of the cold water thirty thousand feet below her she unfolds the paper and reads.

Dear Lily,
This will be my last correspondence with you. It saddens me that the purpose of my writing has shifted so dramatically from self-revelation to the promise of vengeance, as I was enjoying the way the space between us was narrowing with each meeting. This is how it felt for me, anyway.

I can see now how unlikely it was that you and I could have been—been what? What was the nature of the relationship I sought for us to have? Plainly not the father-daughter who might dine together, attend the theater, share discussions of our everyday ups and downs. But we could have had something. Our own accord. Our own kind.

But that is over now.

I will kill you, Lily.

Why is it important for you to know? Because I want every last second of your life to be so scalded by fear that you will come to prefer death by your own hand over deliverance by mine. Yet you will lack the opportunity, if not the courage, to end it that way. Part of you will hold on to the chance that I will show mercy at the end, that despite the evidence for cruelty I have demonstrated you will be different, there will be a word you can say that will give me pause. You would be wrong to think this.

One mistake.

If I had to put into words the expression on the faces of the thousands I have fed upon as their lives drained away, the meaning behind the "death mask" that the psychopaths you once tried to categorize lived to see again and again, it's not merely horror, it's the wish to have done one thing differently. To have taken a different way home. To have not accepted that invitation to come upstairs. To be born in a different place at a different time, to be anyone else so as to avoid the crushing fact of the now.

Your mistake, Lily, was entrusting a group of cowardly mercenaries over me.

You may try to tell yourself that your affections for the one with the scarred face pulled you over to the side of good. But he seeks me as his prize, not you. You are a way to the monster and nothing else. A fuck, perhaps. No man will refuse that if it comes along with the deal.

No matter where you go, I will find you.

You will never lose me, and I will never be far.

Consider this moment for example.

I am onboard this aircraft with you.

Look around you, or not. Try to find me, or not.

You might think, after all this time of killing, that there is no novelty in it for me anymore. But killing you, my only child, how you will first try not to scream, then not stop screaming, and finally fail to find the air to give it voice—it excites me, Lily.

> Yours,
> Client No. 46874-A

PART 3

Unbound

40

Once they touch down and everyone is jamming the aisles so they can wait in an unmoving conga line for another ten minutes, Lily does what she told herself not to and looks for him.

He's on the plane, but she can't spot him. He wants to stretch her terror tight before making his appearance, which could be in the terminal, could be anywhere.

Once she's off the plane, she considers heading straight for the bathroom and hiding in one of the stalls but can only picture him leaning against the opposite wall when she came out. Going forward is the only strategy that can give her time. Constant movement.

Figuring he'll expect her to take a taxi into the city she heads for the shuttle bus instead. There's a terrible five minutes when she's sitting at the back waiting for the driver to close the door, watching the passengers show their tickets one after the other.

She sinks in her seat and peers out her window.

Go, she mentally urges the driver. *Just . . . fucking . . . go.*

A moment later the doors sigh shut and they're moving, joining the flow of traffic on the curving lanes and onto the expressway. Even now she looks for him. Every Town Car a rear window to be lowered to show his face. Every rental a horn to be tooted as he drove up next to them.

She gets out at Penn Station. She figures that going by bus lends the advantage of jumping from one to another, not to mention the presence of witnesses. He'll want to be alone with her. If pressed he'll do it fast and in front of hundreds, but he would prefer to savor it, just the two of them.

When she stands at the ticket window Lily takes a moment to decide where to go first and picks the milk run to Buffalo. At some point she'll have to find a computer to discover where the safe house is but right now it's time to move.

She dozes for a stretch after Utica and when she wakes decides to go all the way to the final stop. There, in the Buffalo station, she buys a chocolate donut and a can of Hawaiian Punch, and borrows a laptop from a pierced girl in a Dead Kennedys T-shirt. Once she downloads the one file on the USB stick she turns the screen away so that she's the only one who can read what's there.

18 DAWSON DRIVE, FARO, YUKON TERRITORY, CANADA

Lily brings up a map and enters the address, reads the Wiki entry that appears under the town's name. A mining outpost about a five-hour drive northeast of Whitehorse, once thriving but now mostly abandoned.

She returns the laptop to the pierced girl and heads into the bathroom where she flushes the USB stick into the sewers. Where she's headed is in her head alone now. There's no way to find her unless you could fish the address directly from her brain. Starting now, she knows the one after her is working to do exactly that.

41

She crosses the continent on the Trans-Canada Highway, first through the endless dips and rises over the hunchback of Lake Superior and then across the flats of the prairies, the snow-dusted fields stretching to the horizon until it gives up and lets the gunmetal sky take over. Lily gets off only to use the bathroom or buy convenience store food, urging the bus to go faster past the signs for Moose Jaw and Medicine Hat, names she'd find funny if she wasn't so scared.

At Calgary she decides to fly the rest of the way. Once she lands in Whitehorse there's no option other than to acquire a vehicle. She heads to a bank downtown and secures a certified check that buys her a used Ford F-150 pickup. After she grabs extra jerricans of gas, water, and a box of granola bars she's out of there, speeding north.

Her lack of sleep has her seeing things. A figure running alongside her truck through a burnt forest. An animal—a white horse—standing in the middle of the road as she comes over a rise. The worst of them all is when she spots the girl. A tiny body in an unzipped winter coat lying at the side of the road. But as she nears, she sees it's not a girl, not her six-year-old self, but a gutted bag of garbage.

There's little snow given the time of year and when she turns off onto the road to Faro she's grateful for it. How had her mother managed in country like this, through whole winters like this? The answer was she never left. Once the snow came the two of them lived on canned food and powdered milk, choosing sanctuary over access to the world outside.

It still wasn't far enough. Even there, the monster had found them.

She comes into town in darkness, her headlights revealing the power generator building, the grocery store the only operating tenant in the strip mall, the rows of town houses built in a rush years ago. There's only a handful of windows with the lights on inside. One of them shows the outline of a woman who looks out at her with curiosity.

Even in the dark Lily can see that the town

was constructed and vacated with equal haste. The residences virtually identical in appearance, the few amenities—the baseball diamond, gas station, school—all closed. She finds the address without having to look for it. One moment she's doing a circle of the town's perimeter and the next she's on Dawson Drive. Number 18 the same unloved unit as the others with the sole exception of a working yellow bulb over the number.

She parks in the back. There's only two other vehicles there with hers—another pickup and an older Jeep Cherokee—and judging from the neat carpet of snow around them neither has been recently used. She steps out of the truck and locks it. The automatic beep of its horn startles her so badly it almost brings her to her knees.

Once inside she spends a minute debating over whether to turn on the lights. Even if Michael has beaten her here, she can't defend herself very well standing unarmed in the dark. The thermostat is set to fifty-five degrees. She cranks it to seventy.

It's a sparsely furnished two-bedroom unit with some basic cooking utensils and pans in the kitchen and a single towel in the bathroom. The only remarkable things about the place are the weapons she finds in the master bedroom's closet. A Sauer hunting rifle, Beretta handgun, a Mossberg 12-gauge pump-action shotgun, along with ample ammunition.

On the kitchen table, just as Will told her, there's a satellite phone with one number programmed into it. She dials without thinking.

"Lily?"

She's so surprised to hear Will's voice—to hear someone address her by name—her throat tightens. "You're alive!"

"I lost him. I was close and I lost him. He must have dug the GPS out of his arm somehow, because he—"

"Where are you?"

"Chicago."

"Why there?"

"It's the best place to fly out of to get to wherever you are."

She tells him where she is. How Michael was on her flight from Amsterdam but that she hasn't seen him since.

"Don't go outside," he says. "Don't do anything. I'm coming."

Lily moves her eyes from the front door to the curtains pulled over the living room window to the back door.

"Will?"

"Yeah?"

"Hurry."

42

Frozen waffles. A dry bowl of Froot Loops. A can of fruit cocktail.

Lily's breakfast is a five-year-old's dream and she eats it hungrily, coming away with a sugar high. Next up, a shower. She watches the water spiral down the drain, the days of travel peeling off her in discolored suds.

There's no clothes in any of the drawers so Lily is forced to put what she was wearing into the wash. It's how she ends up catching sight of her naked self in the mirror loading slugs into the shotgun.

Well look at you now, her inner voice congratulates her.

That's when the doorbell rings.

There's no way Will could've gotten here from Chicago so fast.

Lily wraps a towel around herself and, bringing the Mossberg with her, goes down the hall to stand five feet from the door. The shotgun leans against her shoulder and the barrel is set dead center.

"Who's there?"

She hears something from the other side but it's too quiet to make out.

"Who's *there?*"

"Jim," a male voice says, louder this time. "Jim

Hurst. Your neighbor? I'm at number fourteen?"

Lily tiptoes to the window, pulls the curtain back an inch. She can't see anything other than a single set of boot prints leading up the walk.

She returns to the door and readies the shotgun again. Stepping forward she unlocks it.

"Okay. Door's open."

Nothing happens. Then she notices the knob turning. With a nudge, the door whispers open.

"Oh shit," the man says when he sees Lily holding the shotgun.

"Are you alone?"

"Divorced."

"I mean is there anyone with you out there?"

The man looks at the empty street. "Out *here?* No."

"Okay," Lily says, and lowers the weapon. The man's attention diverts to the fact she's wearing only a towel.

"Maybe I came at a bad time."

"It's not the best."

"I just noticed your vehicle out back and wanted to say hello," he says. "We don't get many new people here at this time of year. Or any time of year."

Lily says nothing.

"So. You need anything, like I said, I'm down at number fourteen," Jim Hurst wraps up, reaching for the doorknob.

"I appreciate that," Lily says, then remembers

she needs to be invisible. "Jim, would you mind not telling anyone else I'm in this unit? My husband is coming, and I want to surprise him."

"Surprise him," the man repeats before he closes the door. "Bet you'd be good at that."

43

Lily spends the rest of the day looking out the front and back windows and confirming the safety is off on the shotgun a thousand times. She takes a long while deciding where to position herself to shoot if Michael tries to come in. She decides on a chair she pulls from the wobbly dining room table, setting it up between the carpeted living room and tiled entrance hall, so that she has a shot at the front door, back door, or bay window. Even if he gets in through a point of entry on the second floor she's got the base of the stairs covered too.

What she hadn't counted on was how hard it is to sit in a crappy chair for hours on end trying to remain ready to blow someone's head off. It's not long before her butt hurts, her head hurts, everything hurts.

Will would help. They could take turns keeping watch. Maybe they could do some other things together too.

She makes a mental note to make sure it's not

Will trying to get into the house before she blows a hole through his chest, and she's etching this thought into the muscles of her arms that hold the shotgun against her like a swaddled infant—*Don't shoot Will*—when Lily falls asleep.

She's kissing. Being kissed.

Her eyes open and she immediately searches for the shotgun on her lap or propped against her side.

It's gone.

"Fuck. *Fuck!*"

She's about to rush upstairs to get another gun from the closet when she sees a man holding the Mossberg sitting on the living room sofa.

"I let myself in," Will says.

"You scared the shit out of me."

"This place is remote, no question about it. But the locks? Not so great."

Lily knew she would be happy if she ever saw Will again. But now that he's here, she's even happier than she guessed.

"Were you kissing me in my sleep?" she asks.

"No," he says. "But it seemed like a good dream you were having."

"It was."

"Been a while since I had one of those."

"A dream or a kiss?"

Will smiles at this but doesn't answer, which is an answer in itself.

After having something to eat Will tells her how he lost Michael soon after Romania and knew he would be after Lily, and that she was most likely to return to the States.

"Do you know where he is now?" she asks.

"No. But with you here—with the two of us here—we must be like a lighthouse for him."

"So what do we do?"

"We make our stand. There's no point in running anymore."

The two of them sit looking at each other across the round dining room table, trying to guess the other's thoughts.

"Frankenstein, Jekyll and Hyde, Dracula," Lily says. "They're him. He's where all of them came from."

"That wasn't in our file."

"I think I'm the only person he's ever told. Aside from my mother, I suppose."

"Why are you telling me this?"

"Because when we kill him, we'll be killing history. Because part of those stories are true, and once he's gone, they'll just be stories again."

Will leans back in his chair. "Are you having second thoughts? You need to tell me now."

"That's not what I'm saying."

"What are you saying, exactly?"

"That I'm the only one to know everything about him."

"The world doesn't have to know everything," he says. "Most of the time the world is better off *not* knowing."

She feels him then. A presence stronger than any previous twinge. He's flying toward this place and will be here soon.

"You want to go upstairs?" Lily asks Will.

"Like the bedroom upstairs?"

"Yes."

He stands, pulling the rifle off the table.

"Let's bring both guns," he says.

44

Afterward, lying on the bed in the otherwise unfurnished bedroom, they tell each other secrets.

For Will, it's the people he's had to kill in the service of his country and, more recently, for money. "People say stuff like that keeps you up at night," he tells her. "But I sleep fine. The thing that bothers me is that it *doesn't* bother me. Maybe I'm missing that part."

"Maybe I am too," Lily says.

She tells him about how she's always felt estranged from others, as if she was studying people instead of being one herself. For a long time she supposed this was a side effect from her mother dying when she was so young, or the baby she lost after always being sure she never wanted one. But now, since meeting Michael, she's not so sure about any of these explanations.

"That hole in my life—what if it's who I am?" she asks, stroking the length of his arm. "What if that's my father's character? In me?"

It's the first time she's said any of this out loud. Before he can react, the doorbell rings.

"Stay here." Will jumps out of bed and pulls on his jeans.

"We go together," she says, putting on her clothes and picking the Mossberg up off the floor.

Downstairs, Will hangs back with the rifle pointed at the door. He motions for Lily to look out the front window.

"It's the neighbor," she whispers. "It's okay."

Will leans the rifle against the kitchen wall just out of sight and Lily does the same with the shotgun in the living room corner.

The doorbell rings again.

Lily unlocks it and turns the knob.

Jim Hurst stands on the front stoop. He's as far back as the cement platform allows, so that he looks as though he wants to toss something inside before making a run for it. It also leaves him mostly in darkness, the light from the entry hall falling on his boots but not making it as far as his face.

"Jim?" Lily says, and the man steps forward.

He looks between Lily and Will. "Your husband made it," he says.

Will comes closer and stands in front of Lily so that he fills the doorframe. He looks both ways down the empty street. "Can we help you?"

"Something's wrong," Hurst says.

"What is it?"

"I went to the market to buy some cigarettes and—oh Christ."

Will holds the man by the shoulder when it seems he's about to pass out.

"What about the market?" Will asks.

"It was Ella. The lady who works nights. She was . . . in *pieces*." Hurst looks to Lily. "He said a bear did it."

"Who said that?"

"The man."

Hurst shifts nervously between the two of them, as if he's failed in a way he doesn't yet recognize.

"Was he a police officer?" Will asks.

"If he was, he wasn't in uniform."

"What did he say to you?" Lily asks.

"He told me to warn people about the bear. Go door-to-door. Asked if I knew any renters who recently came into town. Only person I could think of was you."

Will steps around Hurst and gives the street a thorough look. The rooftops too.

"That man you spoke to isn't with the police," Will says, coming back inside.

"Who the hell is he then?"

"He's on the wrong side of things."

Hurst nods as if he understands.

"Go home. Get inside and lock the doors," Will tells him. "Don't come out again no matter what you see or hear."

The man nods again, but stops at the bottom step, turns. "What're you going to do?"

"Kill him," Will says, and closes the door.

45

Lily retrieves the Mossberg and waits for Will to move away from the door.

"He's here," Lily says.

"Yeah."

"He knows where we are."

Will looks at her. "It's okay," he says. "We want him to come."

Will motions for her to sit on the floor. When she's there, he sits next to her, so that they're back to back.

"You've got the rear door. I've got the front," he says.

"How long are we going to sit here?"

"Until it's over."

Even before Jim Hurst told them about the man at the Faro grocery store, Lily knew Michael was here. Not the monster in the cell in Romania, but the man-who's-not-a-man. He'd been the man she'd known during their meetings together at least as long as it took to write the letter he'd left for her on the plane, but he'd changed back at some point in his pursuit of her. She knows now the line between the one and the other is unreliable, ready to give way in an instant.

She closes her eyes and reaches out to Michael, visualizing where he might be, but all she picks up is an ocean of black oil. He's hiding from her. The thing beneath the surface, waiting to pull her under.

"Lily?"

"Yeah?"

"We do this right, I'm thinking a vacation."

"Like a rest-of-our-lives, running-from-assassins kind of vacation?"

"Guess it better be one of those."

"How about Samoa?"

"Why there?"

"You know Robert Louis Stevenson? Jekyll and Hyde? It's where he—"

Something slams against the back door so hard it almost pops off its hinges.

"Do it, Lily," Will tells her. "Do it now!"

Lily slips her finger around the trigger. Just how her mother taught her. Except she won't hesitate this time. Once she sees it, she'll take it down.

She's setting her cheek against the side of the gun when she hears the scream.

A man. Outside the back door. A terrified wailing she recognizes as Jim Hurst's.

"Help me! *Please!*"

Will is on his feet.

"It's a trap," she says.

"If it is, let's set it off."

46

Will rushes out the back door, following Jim Hurst's screams, and is halfway across the parking area by the time Lily makes it outside.

She goes after him down an icy slope and slips, the shotgun flung from her hands. By the time she gets to her feet again and grabs the Mossberg she catches only a glimpse of Will as he passes through the space between another pair of town house blocks. She runs with her head down against the freshly falling snow, each flake biting her skin.

Beyond the town houses is the baseball diamond she noticed when she first drove into town. As she approaches, she sees three men in front of the backstop fence. Michael is holding Jim Hurst, his arm around his neck. Will is thirty feet away with his rifle raised.

Lily stops at the border between the frozen

grass and hard infield. Michael sees her. Shows his silver teeth in a jagged grin.

"We're all here," he says.

He takes a long stride closer to her, the hold on Jim's throat so tight he's incapable of speech, of breath.

"Let him go," Will says.

"I remember you," Michael says, moving his gaze from Lily to Will. "Your sister too."

Will's fury freezes him. Every part of his body set to explode except his mind, held rigid on the man's words.

"The younger the better, I've found," Michael goes on. "Of course, it must have been *awful* for you."

He moves closer. So relaxed it's easy to forget how quickly he traverses the distance. Now, Michael is in front of Will. Then he comes straight and fast, his feet barely touching the ground as he flies forward.

"No!"

Will fires, but Lily's voice is a distraction that, even at this close range, diverts the shot from where he'd aimed. The bullet travels through Jim Hurst's shoulder rather than Michael's face.

Lily watches as Hurst's swollen lips move but no sound comes out. It looks to her as if he's practicing a kiss.

Will fires again.

This time he hits Hurst in the leg, going

through his thigh and Michael's too, though only the former appears to feel it. Hurst is spasming now, the shock inducing a seizure that looks all the more unnatural because no part of him is touching the ground. A marionette held up by a puppet master who barrels both of them forward.

Hurst's body slams into Will before he gets off another shot.

It knocks him onto his back, the rifle flipping end over end. When he tries to scramble to where the weapon lies, Michael drops Hurst on top of him, so that for a moment the two men are struggling to untangle their limbs. When Will gets an arm free he makes a move to pull the pistol from the holster at his waist. Before he reaches it Michael kicks his wrist so hard it breaks with an audible snap.

The shotgun, Lily tells herself. *You're holding it.*

She raises the butt and aims at Michael. It's dark, even darker in this moment than the one that preceded it, and her entire body is shaking from something other than the cold. But she's armed the Mossberg with slugs to take out targets up close and she can't get any closer than she is now.

Michael pauses to look directly at her, a gaze so unguarded and clear there's no choice but to return it. He looks at her with the longing of a man memorizing his lover's shape before he leaves her for good.

And then, before he speaks, before she can fire, he changes.

From Michael to Hyde. He to it.

The monster lifts Will up by his broken wrist and brings his throat to its mouth. The teeth clamp down. Pushing through the skin.

"No!"

Lily pulls the trigger but she's stumbling backward and the shot goes wide. She pumps out the shell and brings another into the chamber.

Once. It only has to be once.

She aims square at the thing's chest.

Even as she fires it's moving, bending to avoid the slug. Untouched.

Lily pumps the used cartridge out again and takes in a new one. Only now does she see that when it moved to avoid her shot it brought Will up with it, holding him drained and twitching, his face a blank.

The thing waits until she's looking at it again. Then it swings its clawed hand up to stick all five of its blades into Will's side, throws him over its shoulder, and comes at her.

Lily turns. Tells her legs to move but they only half comply, the knees spongy, the thighs heavy. With every contact of her feet with the ground she expects to feel the blades slicing into her back.

She knows it's a mistake even as she pauses to look back. But she looks anyway. The thing is so close she won't have time to start up the slope before it reaches her. Even as she watches, it lurches forward, Will bouncing over its shoulder.

She brings the shotgun up. Fires.

The thing staggers back and Lily sees it: a semicircle of blood just above its hip. It touches its free hand to the wound. Looks up at her and utters a sound at once animal and mechanical. A wolf howl combined with the shriek of a chain saw.

Lily starts up the slope toward the town house's parking lot. She's almost at the top and thinks of shooting again but she's not sure how many slugs she has left. Two. Maybe only one. Maybe none.

Get to the car. Get in and drive.

She makes it to the parking lot and glances back. The thing spits a wad of mucus and blood that melts a dark circle into the snow. Then it starts toward her.

Her keys. Where are her keys? She finds the metal loop in her pocket and unlocks the door.

The thing makes the top of the slope, drops Will's body to the ground.

Lily jumps in the pickup and closes the door just as the thing slams against it, clawing at the door handle.

She starts the engine and jams it into revers

without looking, straightening to go out the driveway to the road. But the thing is with her the whole way. Scraping at her windshield, its clawed hand dragging along the door, a screech of metal like something alive and suffering.

The truck jumps forward. Lily checks the rearview mirror.

The monster is there, swinging Will's body by his ankles as if he weighed no more than a bag of laundry. Its teeth crack together before it erupts into a new howl of hysterical laughter, or fury, or grief. Except it isn't any of those things. A sound empty of any human feeling at all.

47

Lily crosses the border from Canada into Alaska as the dawn appears like a gray ribbon behind the hills.

Other than presenting her fake passport to the customs officer she stops only to pour the extra jerricans of gas into the tank. The road is patchy with black ice, so that anything faster than forty mph risks spinning her into the ditch.

She figures she has a bubble of time to get ⁊here she's going without the thing catching up ⁺h her. After she gunned it out of Faro, it would ` had to find a vehicle and keys to match. ℮ ⁊neant breaking into one of the inhabited town houses first. It probably meant more killing too. And though she knew her shot wasn't direct enough to have brought it down, it would have at least been slowed by its wounds.

There would have been no way it could have caught up with her on the road out before she made the Klondike Highway. After that, there were any number of side roads she could have ducked down, places she could have hidden and waited.

She might have even had a chance of escaping altogether if it didn't already know where she's going.

The miles between Tetlin Junction and Dot Lake are so similar Lily is sure she'll have trouble spotting the lumber road that leads to the cabin. Yet when she comes over another rise like the hundred rises before it she sees it right away: no signpost, no gate, just a cut into the stumpy trees to the south.

She takes the turn and, a few miles along, finds the trail still there: rough and so narrow the branches slash at her windows, but used frequently enough by moose hunters to still allow a 4x4 in.

After another mile and a half it stops. The bush grown across the gap, the birch and spruce branches tangled in a web. Lily grabs the Mossberg and a water bottle and starts hiking the rest of the way, which, by her guess, should be just over another mile or so.

When she makes it out the clearing is broader than she remembers. The absence of the high grasses of summer leaves it looking bald, so that the cabin sits in the center as an anomaly, its slanting roof and trapezoid window frames a small protest of the man-made against the chaos of forest.

She's surprised to find the door still on its hinges. This, along with other indications of repair, shows that the cabin's occasional visitors do enough to prevent it from collapsing.

Inside it's dark. Once her eyes adjust she can see there's still a kitchen and a table with plates holding nothing but mouse turds, a few wooden chairs randomly situated as if the last people here had left at the sound of an alarm.

The first thing she does is check the shotgun and utter an involuntary moan when she finds only one slug.

That's all you'll need.

She makes sure the safety's off and takes a long drink of water.

Just hit it where it counts.

Now that she's here, Lily expects her nerves to take over, to keep her alert. Instead, the weight of fatigue has her pacing around the cabin, fighting to string together the simplest thoughts. Where should she position herself? Stay by a window and keep watch, or wait for it to come in? In the end she doesn't make a decision. She slumps to the floor next to what was once her childhood bedroom, her back to the wall.

The body has its limits. The mind too. You live through enough panic and horror to never sleep again but sleep comes nevertheless, unwanted and suffocating as a wool hood pulled over your head.

Lily's eyes close without her noticing.

She dreams of blood.

Swimming in an ocean of it, thick and undulating in sluggish waves. So heavy it's hard to keep her head up to breathe. But she has to. There's an urgent need to keep slapping her arms forward that goes beyond preventing herself from drowning. There's someone out here with her in the endless crimson sea.

Lily? What are you doing?

She hears her mother calling for her and swims toward the voice.

Stop it. Stop this now.

When she finds her mother she's fighting to stay above the surface. Her hair glued to her skull, her teeth pale as Chiclets.

Lily! No!

Her mother's eyes are filled not with relief at seeing Lily but with horror. It doesn't prevent what Lily does next, doesn't give her pause to ask herself why.

She reaches out to her mother, puts her hands on the crown of her head, and pushes her under. Holds her down. Lily feels the vibration of her mother's body swallowing and choking and swallowing again until she sinks away and the ocean is still as a mirror.

She's awakened by the monster knocking at the door.

48

Three thuds. Each followed by the hollow scratch of knuckles dragged over wood. Just as her mother had done after the third knock years ago, Lily rises and goes to the door.

"Michael?"

Deeper silence.

She presses her cheek against the door and can feel it on the other side: arms at its sides, shoulders hunched, head cocked.

For it to work, it will have to go fast: unlock the door, take two steps back, blow a hole through its chest. Three actions compressed into one.

She unlocks the door. Takes two steps back. Raises the shotgun level and fits the butt against her shoulder.

The door opens not by force but on its own, a slow widening. Its bottom stroked over the floor by licks of frigid air from outside.

She should fire now. Now. *Now.*

"Will?"

It steps forward and the floorboards utter a worried groan at the weight. The eyes roll in their sockets, holding on her a moment and then spinning away. The mouth opens and clamps shut, the lips smack together. The reflex of biting and chewing being tested before the real thing.

Like the women Michael had offered to Stoker in the rented room in Soho or the series of failed experiments, the brides he'd attempted to make before he'd found Lily's mother, this is Will in resemblance only, alive only in the capacity to move and kill and eat. For the first time, his scarred and misshapen face matches the monstrosity of the rest of him.

"Please don't," she says at the same time she takes aim.

It answers by coming forward. One foot and then the other, every new step more sure than the one before.

"Four trees."

A noise escapes its mouth. It tries again. They could be words, they could be nothing at all.

"More ease."

It's little more than a body length away when Lily hears it clearly.

"Forgive me."

She pulls the trigger.

49

The thing that was once Will staggers back. Lily drops the shotgun from the shock of the noise only after watching the thing look down at its chest, the eyes momentarily focusing on the blood soaking through its parka.

It places a hand over the wound and presses, not to stanch the bleeding but to push its hand inside, feeling around its spine, searching for something dropped into a pool of brackish water.

It looks up at her again. Then it falls sideways onto the floor and goes still.

Lily bends to pick up the shotgun but realizes it's useless now. There's little chance there's a weapon in the cabin. It doesn't stop her from looking. Under the sink there's a cast-iron pan. On a shelf an unopened can of baked beans. She considers taking each but ends up leaving both where they are.

What's the plan, Doctor? You going to psychoanalyze him to death?

She peers out the open door to the clearing and the woods beyond it. She can't see him but she knows Michael's out there, watching her.

He'll smell you if he doesn't see you, track you if he doesn't smell you. He'll read your mind.

"Why don't you shut up if you don't have any ideas," she hisses.

But I do have an idea.

Thirty years ago, her mother told her where to go. There couldn't be anything at the trailer by the creek to help her now but she has to believe there was a reason she called it the secret place. If nothing else, trying to get there will prevent Lily from dying here, on the same spot, the same floorboards her mother died.

She retreats behind the doorframe and out of view. It won't be full dark for another few hours, she guesses. Does she stay where she is and wait for the night? If she's going to make a run to the trailer—a run anywhere—it will be impossible without at least some sunlight, but she judges that a few shades more of winter dusk might help act as cover.

It gives her time to find a screwdriver in one of the kitchen drawers and pry the plywood off the window in the bedroom. This is where her mother and Lily shared a bed a lifetime ago, cuddled close in the mornings when the warmth of the stove had died down over the night hours. Where she'd watched him stand over her mother's body.

The thought of this and what he's done to Will refreshes her hatred. It doesn't matter if he was anticipating these feelings from her, if he was detecting her rage right now, brightly shining around her like a spotlight. She's done with controlling herself. She hates him and she lets herself hate him. The heat of it tingles through her, anesthetizing her, so that when she crawls out the window frame and cuts her forearm on a shard of glass she barely recognizes it as pain.

There's no obvious entry into the bush, but she thinks she can feel her way through to where the trailer ought to be. When she's twenty yards in she stops to listen, looks back the way she's come. Nothing. But she knows Michael is close. This is the prolonged end he promised her and it hasn't even started yet.

She pulls aside a curtain of thorny devil's club and comes out into a clearing smaller than the one in which the cabin sits.

The trailer is still there. More rust than when she last saw it when she came here some years ago, and its balance atop the four stacks of cinder blocks at its corners more precarious, but still a solid thing that might be entered without it collapsing under your feet.

She loops her fingers through the hole where the doorknob used to be. Up a couple of steps and she's inside.

Lily scans the trailer's interior and finds the derelict mess she expected. Empty plywood cupboards, corroded tins, a Formica table screwed into the paneled wall, a water-plumped paperback of *Steppenwolf.* The ammonia of animal urine strong as smelling salts under her nose.

Why would her mother send her to this place? There's nothing here to defend herself with, nowhere to hide. Whatever she had in mind is gone now.

Unless it was never here to begin with, psycho.

Lily remembers the afternoon as a child she found her mother lying on the ground outside the trailer. She'd always assumed she discovered her mother in the middle of doing something she wished to keep private. But what if she'd *wanted* Lily to find her there? What if she was meant to wonder what her mother had left for her, to find it when she was old enough to see the secret was meant for her?

She goes outside, lies on her back, and slides under the trailer, pushing snow aside with her hands. Once her whole body is under it's easier to move but she worries that even the slightest touch of its underbelly could knock out one of its supports and crush her.

The underside is a patchwork of plywood, squares of steel screwed in here and there to cover rotted holes, a pair of corroded rods running the length of the structure to hold it up. Lily arches her head, shifts to the side to see around her feet. Nothing.

But then: something odd nailed into the trailer's floor.

A wooden box.

Lily recognizes it. A simple pine square with a

locked lid that she recalls her mother once pulling out of a pillowcase she kept in her luggage.

"What's in it?" she had asked.

"Your grandparents' ashes," her mother had answered. Lily didn't want to ask more and risk making her mother upset.

She slithers over to it and finds the box. Without tools there's no way she could free it. The screwdriver. The one she'd used to get out the cabin window. Still in her pocket.

She wedges the screwdriver between the lock and the box's latch. Tugs down.

"Fuck!"

The pain comes with the jerking motion. Her finger feels broken. The good news is the latch seemed to move. A few more yanks on it might pull it out altogether.

She withdraws the index finger that's already swelling and replaces it with her middle finger. This time she reaches her left arm over to grasp the wrist of the right to bring the screwdriver down with greater force.

Two broken fingers is better than waiting for him to pull you out of here.

She counts herself down from three then tugs as hard as she can.

With a metallic pop the latch tears free from the wood and the door swings open. A plastic bag clatters onto her chest.

Ashes don't clatter.

She pulls the bag off her and looks inside. A pair of gloves with curved metal talons for fingers. A set of silver teeth. The points sharpened, the cuspids long as surgical needles.

She hunted with them.

The secret of the secret place.

She left them for you.

Lily shimmies back the way she came, pulling the bag with her. Her index finger strobing in pain. Glancing at it she sees the ninety-degree angle at its knuckle. The swelling has spread to her entire hand, now rounded and hard as a baseball.

Once she's out from under the trailer she lies there, scanning the trail and surrounding bush. No movement, no fresh tracks. She gets to her feet, slides her back along the side of the trailer to the door, and opens it. It squeaks so loudly she almost closes it again but figures there's no option but to go inside.

Up the couple of stairs she pulls the door closed and looks around for something to lock it with. The best she can do is tie a fragment of rope left on the kitchen counter through the hole where the handle used to be and knot the other end to the pipe under the sink. It won't be anywhere near enough to stop the thing if it tries to get in, but it may give her some time.

Lily creeps away from the door, bent low to avoid being seen through the small window frames long smashed clear of glass. Once she makes it to the back she opens the bag and pulls its contents out.

It's all in surprisingly good shape: the leather of the gloves and the tightening straps at the wrist still supple and strong, the blades so sharp they leave a cut in her thumb when she touches one.

50

She starts with the teeth. It takes a couple of tries to figure out they don't slide in but fit over the existing teeth until they click and grip around the rear molars. She puts one glove on her unswollen left hand. It fits perfectly, the leather snug and smooth.

There's a fragment of mirror left on the wall of the bathroom stall and she gets up to inspect her face in the glass.

You look good. Like your mother.

Something bumps against the outside wall of the trailer. The structure whimpers, shifting on its moorings.

It's here. Peter Farkas's demon. Mr. Hyde. Yet Michael is here too. His voice finds its way to her, speaking in her head.

Do you see what you are yet, Lily? Do you see what you did?

She's expecting another bump against the wall. Instead, the monster drags its claws along the length of the trailer all the way to the door.

Your mother tried to cure you. Remember? The teas and broths she made you eat? The strange songs she sang? Some of them lullabyes. But others chants, spells. She tried to banish the unnatural from your soul and keep you human.

Lily staggers out of the stall. All at once the screeching stops. She tastes the bitter spoonfuls her mother fed her, calling it soup though Lily knew it wasn't. And the words her mother murmured as Lily choked and swallowed—that was magic. That was a light that wanted to chase the darkness out of her.

But you didn't want the darkness out of you, did you? Not all of it. You wanted to be your father's child. So how did you make her stop, Lily?

Outside the trailer the monster grunts. The satisfied sound of an animal that knows its prey is trapped.

Lily's head is full of the dream of blood, the memory of her six-year-old self kneeling over the body. She did it. She fired a bullet through her mother's chest with the Remington she'd been taught to use.

"No!"

It was meant to be a warning only, to get her mother to stop trying to change who she was. She was a child who was learning she wasn't merely a child, not merely like everyone else in the world, and it frightened her. Excited her.

"No!"

She sees her mother's eyes, wide in front of her.

"Please, baby! No!"

Lily pulled the trigger. And then, to be sure it was done, to make her mother stop staring into her, stop judging, she had taken the hunting knife in her tiny hand and brought it down.

When I came through the door, Alison's body was on the floor. I knew what had happened, I could see it in your face. So I let the thing inside me show itself. Tore into Alison's body even though she was already dead. To make it look like a bear did it. And you? Your head came around the corner. And you watched.

The claws tap against the metal skin of the trailer. A thousand scratches gouging through then pulling back until the wall is perforated and sharp as a cheese grater.

I protected you from the truth, Lily. I made it look like I was the one who did it—made you see a monster and flew you far, far away.

The blades anchor into the trailer's side and cut screaming lines through the steel.

You were a child. My only child. But it's time you see what you did. What you are.

"Stop," Lily whispers.

It's time for me to give you the gift you've come for.

The monster hooks a claw through the open hole where the doorknob used to be and pulls. The door squeaks but the rope holds.

Lily fights the urge to be sick. Her side is pressed against the wall where the blades have cut through so that the thing will have to rip the door open and come up the first step before it sees her.

"My darling girl."

The voice comes from the other side of the trailer's thin metal door.

"Are you ready?"

Yes. You're ready, Lily's inner voice tells her. *Show him just how ready you are.*

A second claw slides through the hole, tightens its grip so that the points of the blades dig into the metal. Heaves it back.

The rope pulls on the pipe under the sink and holds for a quarter second before it comes free and the door flies off its hinges.

Lily blindly brings her left hand down. She's only sure she made contact with her claws when she sees three of the five blades shining with blood.

The monster is there.

It looks down at its chest as Lily backs away. Past the sink, all the way to the rear bench that used to pull out into a bed.

The creature looks up at her. The lips pulled back in a snarling show of teeth.

"You *cut* me."

It comes all the way into the trailer, filling the space of its narrow passageway. Starts toward her.

"That wasn't very nice to do to dear old dad, was it?"

Lily can hear the *swick-swick* of its claws as they slice through the air.

She kneels. There is nowhere to run, no window large enough to squeeze through. It doesn't matter. She doesn't want to get away. A new power surges through her, the thrumming life of horror itself.

"Not nice at all . . ."

It kicks her. The toe of its foot hard to her chest. She's thrown back against the bench, hitting her head on the edge. The blow almost knocks her out. She fights to remain conscious, feels herself swimming to the surface as though she's been upended by a strong wave.

The thing kicks her again.

It wants you to lie down, her voice tells her. *It wants you to have nothing left to fight with and then it will gut you like a fish.*

Lily can see no way to prevent it. She leans against the bench, her legs out straight in front of her. She feels her eyes spinning around. It's why when the monster bends to put its face close to

350

hers she catches only glimpses of it, as though she's on a carousel and sees it only once each revolution.

"I don't know what Michael saw in you," it says.

The eyes are dead. It brings its right claws up slowly to the soft skin at the top of her throat.

"But I'd like to see some of it for myself."

Lily only intends to block its arm with her own but as she wildly swings her left hand up she makes contact with something else. She hears an audible tearing, wet and thick, as the ends of the long blades on her glove catch its skin and cut a line through the side of its throat. There's a pause, an extended moment of frozen soundlessness, before a hot spume fires out of the monster's neck, then another, another. Its life rushing out to the steady rhythm of its heart.

It sees what she's done. The black eyes look around its feet at the rising pool of himself.

It lashes its claws at her and cuts her chest. Lily screams at the instant burning, but she can feel that the wounds aren't deep. She has another chance. Only one.

She uses her teeth this time.

Whether it's from a lack of balance, or it wasn't expecting her to come at it this way, it doesn't block her attack. She bites down into the open wound at its neck. The blood surges into her mouth and she swallows and swallows.

It fights her but she doesn't let go. She can feel its claws slapping and tearing at the back of her jacket but it can't dig into her properly so long as she maintains this embrace, keeps the teeth clenching tighter.

Lily measures its passing in increments of weakness. The abandoned strikes to her back. The quieting of its teeth. Finally, it shudders once and goes still.

Lily spits out the remaining fluid in her mouth. Once more she thinks she's going to be sick but then her stomach calms. It's as if she's ingested a fortifying consommé, comforting and warm, not the crimson glue spilling onto the floor.

A new strength brings her to her feet. She looks down at the thing's body. Is it Hyde or Michael? The eyes are open and vacant, the lips tight over the silver teeth. Part of its features are those of her father, and others the ancient thing within him. She knows that whatever it is, it's dead.

Lily removes the teeth from her mouth and puts them in the pocket of her jacket. The claw-gloves she wraps in a canvas bag she finds under the sink, ties the top with some of the rope she'd used to hold the door closed.

She considers pulling the body out of the trailer and hiding it. The police will find all this in time. They must already be in Faro, looking over Jim Hurst and concluding it was more than a bear attack. Then they'll find Will, and this man in the trailer, neither immediately identifiable. It's the kind of puzzle they'd call outside authorities to help with.

It's all too much to think about. There's the cold to worry her more than the police. There's making it to the road.

Yet she still lingers long enough to notice the journal.

The button on his jacket pocket that had held it inside must have been opened in their struggle, and now the top of its leather cover poked out, the thick string that tied it shut stretched over his chest like a snake.

Lily pulls it out. She winds the string tight around it and the pages inside crinkle like the sound of distant applause. It fits as snug in her pocket as it had in his.

She starts along the trail. How much light is left in the day? She's so disoriented by the events of the past few minutes it's impossible to guess. A couple of hours? Three? All she can do is follow the narrow gap cut through the trees.

After a time she comes upon the crash.

The Jeep Cherokee the thing had taken from the lot in Faro and driven here, smashed into the back of her pickup, totaling them both.

Lily walks on.

He let you do it, her voice says. *Not the thing inside him, not Hyde, but the other part. Michael.*

Now that she hears this she can see no other

explanation. There's no way she should be the one walking out of the bush alive. This was his plan from before he committed the crime that sent him to the Kirby. *Perhaps you could resolve the question of my missing name.* He had threatened her, pursued her, killed before her eyes so that, when the time came, she would defend herself with everything she had. Everything within her that was his that she needed to discover for herself.

He wanted you to swallow his blood.

Lily thinks of something from the books she'd read. What Stoker had one of his vampires say.

The blood is the life! The blood is the life!

And it is.

51

It's almost full night when Lily walks out of the forest. She crawls up the incline out of the ditch and collapses at the side of the road. If she can rest here for a while she might find the strength to walk a few miles more. This is what she tells herself.

You did it. You killed your own mother. It was you.

She keeps her eyes on the road as it slowly rises to the north. The cold is making her sleepy. She fights it by concentrating on the horizon.

The road, the trees.

The horse.

A stallion emerges from the forest a couple hundred yards ahead. Its hide is whiter than the fresh powdering of snow it stands on.

The great animal stops in the middle of the road, looking at her.

If it's a hallucination, she could close her eyes and make it disappear. But when she does so and opens them, it's still there.

Lily raises her arm and waves at it, beckoning. *Come back!*

The horse starts across the road and slips into the trees on the opposite side. Her cheek touches stone as sleep pulls her down.

It's over. She's dying, and it's okay. Michael is gone. The baby. Will. Her mother. No one to return to, no one to be returned.

Before her tears freeze her eyes shut she sees the truck coming over the rise. It eases to a stop next to her. Lily sees spools of wire and an aerial arm in the back. It's an electrical contractor. She's seen them before up here, the mechanical arm used to lift workers to power lines. The driver's door opens and a workman jumps out.

The man approaches her. Her wounds are healing even as she lies here, a prickly tingling, like a team of invisible ants pulling skin together, stitching and smoothing.

He leans over her. He smells like copper.

"What happened to you?"

"There was a man—" she answers, and lets her voice trail off when she realizes there's no way to tell the truth.

"Are you hurt?"

"I think I'm bleeding."

"You better get in the truck. Can you do it on your own?"

"I don't think so."

He scoops her up. The muscled arms feel good under her back. Closer now, she can smell coffee and the doughy sweetness of a donut on his breath.

The driver sets Lily down on the passenger seat and closes the door. He walks around to his side. She watches his deliberate motions and sees how he's a man who thinks in steps. Get the ladder's angle right, make sure the line is grounded, attach the new cable. Except now he's working through a new process. Put the woman in the truck, drive to the hospital in Fairbanks, keep her awake.

They won't find anything until spring if you do it now.

She feels the journal pressing against her left side as if it's a small animal seeking her protection. Later, she will add to it. The end of his story. The beginning of her own.

"You cut anywhere?" the truck driver asks her. "You been shot?"

"No. I'm just . . . scared."

"Well you're okay now. You're safe, all right?"

Lily reaches inside her coat pocket on the right and feels the silver teeth. The sharp points sticky and slick.

The driver avoids looking at her. Lily can feel his concern for her, his fear that she's going to die in his truck. She can hear beyond his interior voice too. His heart. Loud and getting louder.

"You want to listen to the radio?" he asks.

"Sure."

He turns it on. Country and western, just like when she was picked up by a man in a truck on this same road when she was six. Not Randy Travis this time but Ronnie Milsap. "There's No Gettin' Over Me."

The driver turns up the volume but Lily can barely hear it. There's only the man's heart, the deafening passage of blood through his neck. She slips her fingers through the open-mouthed gap of the silver teeth. The driver's eyes fixed on the road ahead.

> Well you can say that you need to be free
> But there ain't no place that I won't be . . .

There's nothing in her head, not a sound or voice or thought. The warm life inside him, whooshing and pounding. So close and ready it's like he's here only for her. A gift.

Acknowledgments

Thanks first to my primary idea bouncer and amazing wife, Heidi Rittenhouse, the best partner in all this a man could ever dream of, and to Maude and Ford, the children who affirm our love and good fortune every day.

I'd say why the following deserve thanks but I'm trying to save a tree or two and in any case they already know: Nita Pronovost, Emily Graff, Jonathan Karp, Marysue Rucci, Kevin Hanson, Anne McDermid, Howard Sanders, Jason Richman, Martha Webb, Chris Bucci, Monica Pacheco, Peter Robinson, Jon Wood, Jemima Forrester, Ben Willis, Amy Prentice, Craig Davidson, Peter McGuigan, Stephanie Cabot, Dominick Montalto, Steven Hayward, Mike Edmonds, and Sarah Knight.

Researching *The Only Child* took me here and there, both in body and books. As to the latter, special mention must be made of the following excellent texts and biographies: *Robert Louis Stevenson* by Claire Harman, *Mary Shelley* by Muriel Spark, *The Poet and the Vampyre* by Andrew McConnell Stott, and *Who Was Dracula?* by Jim Steinmeyer.

About the Author

ANDREW PYPER is the author of seven novels, most recently *The Damned*. *The Demonologist* was a #1 bestseller in his native Canada and won the International Thriller Writers award for Best Hardcover Novel. His other novels include *Lost Girls* (winner of the Arthur Ellis Award and a *New York Times* bestseller), *The Killing Circle* (a *New York Times* Crime Novel of the Year), and *The Guardians* (a *Globe and Mail* Best Book). Three of Pyper's novels are in active development for television or feature film. He lives in Toronto. Visit him at www.andrewpyper.com.

Center Point Large Print
600 Brooks Road / PO Box 1
Thorndike, ME 04986-0001 USA

(207) 568-3717

US & Canada:
1 800 929-9108
www.centerpointlargeprint.com